BAKER BUTCHER DOCTOR DIPLOMAT
Goan Pioneers of East Africa
Selma Carvalho

First published in 2016 by
Selma Carvalho
3 Burlington House
West Drayton UB7 9FE
United Kingdom
http://selmacarvalho.squarespace.com/

Text copyright © Selma Carvalho 2016
Images copyright © named copyright holders

Designed by Nisha Albuquerque
Printed in United Kingdom by Biddles

Acknowledgments

My principal thanks goes to the Melville J. Herskovits Library of African Studies Winterton Collection, Northwestern University; The National Archives, Kew; and the Evangelisch-Lutherisches Missionswerk Leipzig, who all loaned me several images without which this book would not have come to fruition. Joel Bertrand shared with me, for a song, his impressive collection of old East Africa postcards many of which were first published, as if by providence, by late-19th century Goan photographers in Zanzibar. I'm indebted to the British Library and its reading room staff for their many years of patiently dealing with my requests, and the SOAS University Library. My life-long gratitude to the Goan families who let me plunder their family photographs with impunity; Mervyn Maciel and Joseph Pereira de Lord, who I unashamedly mined for information; Richard de Souza, keeper of Goan genealogies; Nisha Albuquerque for the book design; Kurt Bento for his editorial eye; Eddie and Lira Fernandes, my springboard for every initiative since I arrived in London; and Savio and Lauren Carvalho for their enduring love and support.

To Lauren Carvalho
May you wander far

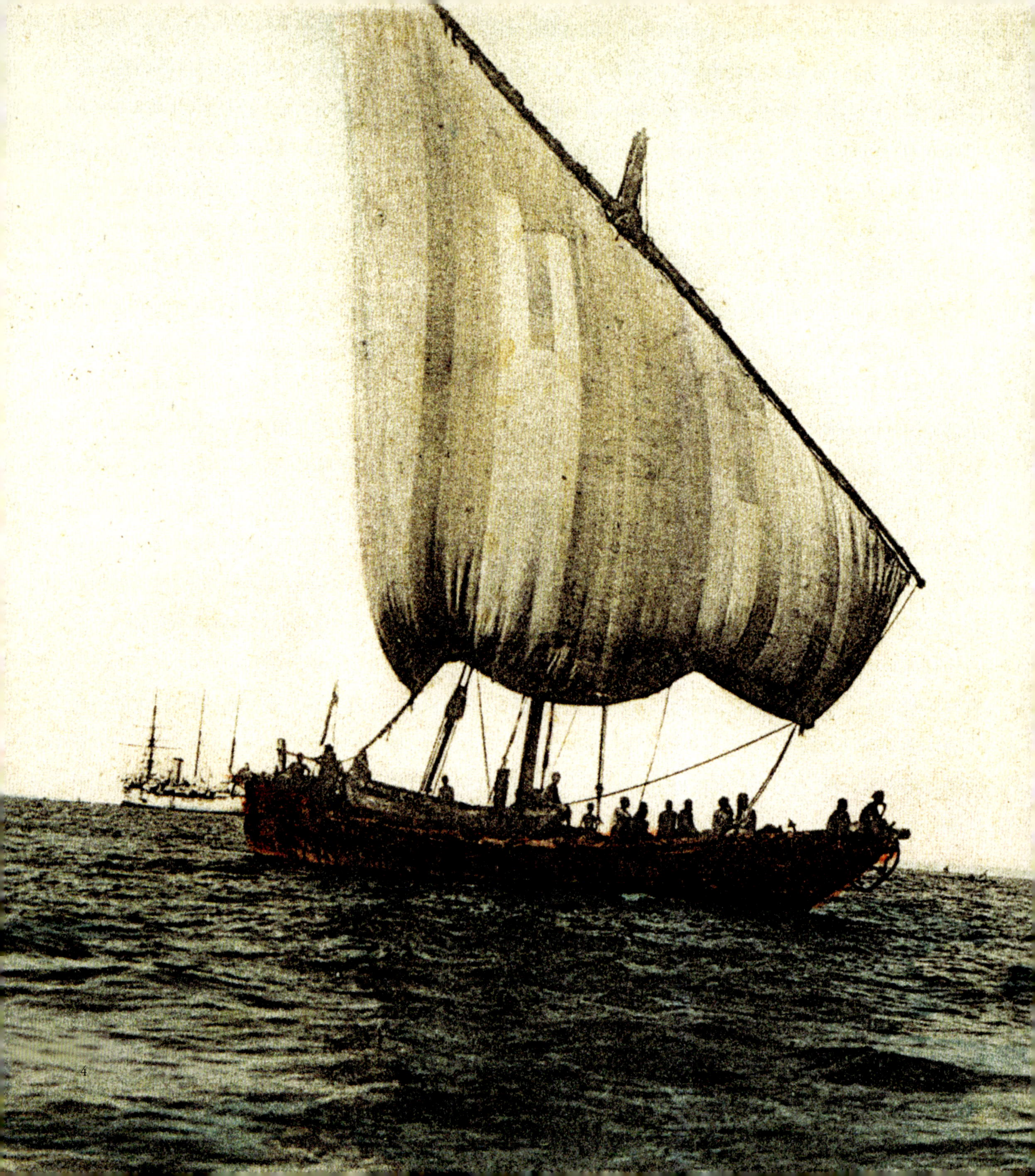

'THE BOLD PIONEER'

'And that true spirit of the British race, which makes the wilderness a dwelling place, and wrestles the desert into fruitful soil; swift on the track of the bold pioneer, science and learning and the arts appear', was the opening cantata inspired by the 1880 Melbourne International Exhibition. Except of course, it was not just the pioneering British engaged in the enterprise of making wilderness liveable. There were other dispersed races - Indians, Arabs, Persians, Jews, Armenians, Chinese, and lesser known perhaps, Goans[1] - instrumental in building new frontier townships.

The Goan contribution, due to lack of scholarship, has been erased from history or worse still, at times, usurped and attributed to colonisers clever with the written word. Preserving this historical narrative requires recovery from fading memories, and finding the rightful place of the bold Goan pioneer in East Africa.

One thing becomes clear on the journey to historical recovery; Goans did not live in the shadow or on the periphery, nor were they always subordinated to colonial interests. They operated with a wide degree of autonomy to manage profitable businesses, offer medical and humanitarian aid, play a diplomatic and philanthropic role, impact infrastructure and shape religious norms. They were in every respect the great frontiersmen venturing into unexplored and often perilous lands, and thriving under precarious conditions. The following pages narrate their role in the early settlement of Zanzibar, Mombasa and Nairobi.

Dhow, Zanzibar, 1905. Most Goan pioneers sailed to East Africa on board dhows. A few arrived by steamer.

[1] A distinction is made between Goans and Indians throughout this book as it was in colonial East Africa.

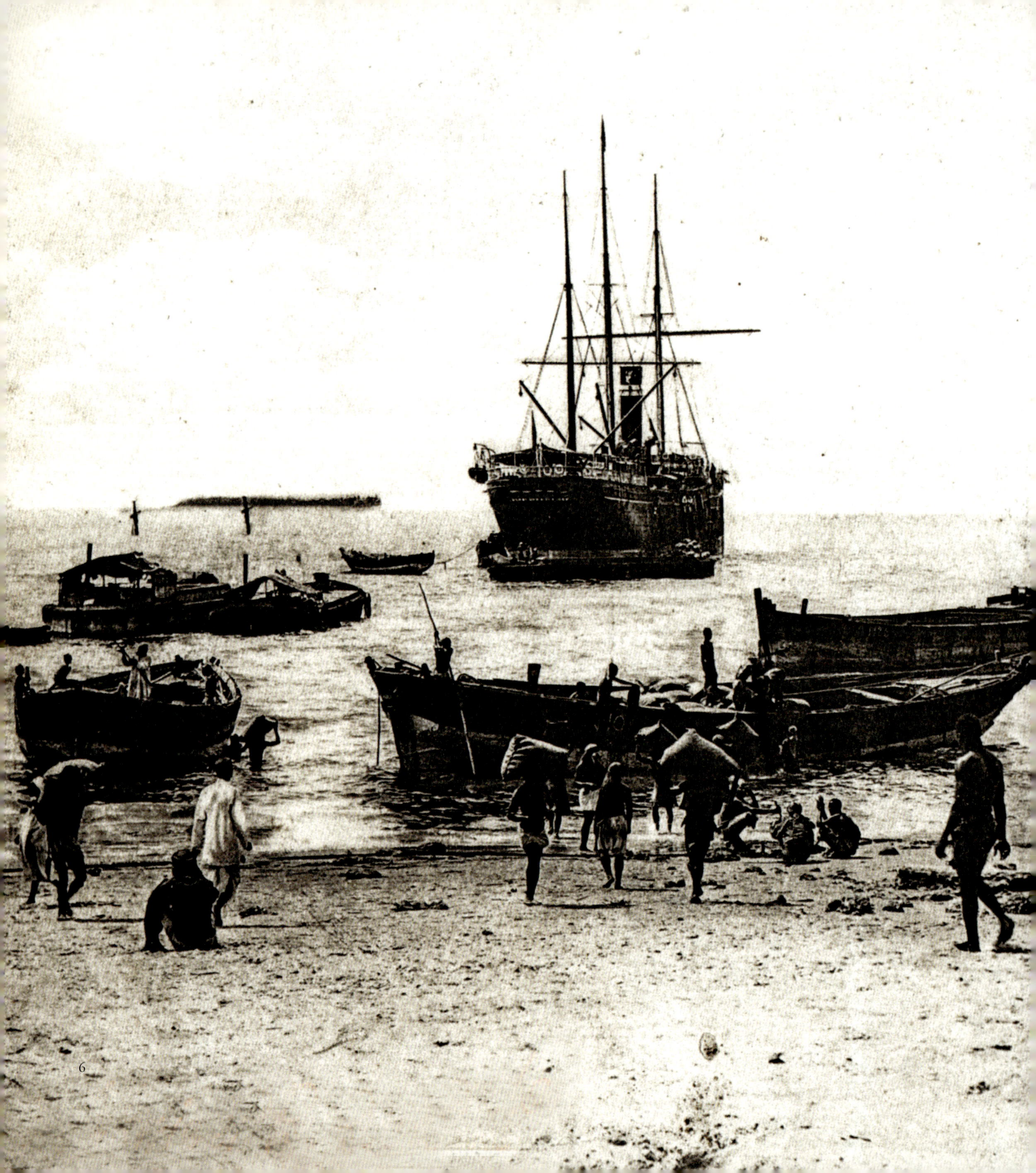

ZANZIBAR
'MAN OF COLOUR': SEAMEN

'The Goans had established themselves on the island of Zanzibar and gradually spread themselves along the coastline opening small store depots, tailoring establishments and bakeries'.

Anonymous letter in the African Standard, 21 November, 1903.

Zanzibar lies on the east coast of Africa separated from India by an ocean of not too inclement tides and trade winds. This clemency had, from the early 19th century, engendered trade between the Omani Arabs who had established a sultanate in Zanzibar and the Kutch on India's west coast. On first sighting Zanzibar from the sea, one noticed, 'the waves break with great violence, and beyond, palms and coconut trees formed a beautiful background'. Once on land, the island seemed less promising. Inhabited by Arab and Indian merchants, African slaves, and a few Europeans, the township made no great pretentions to grandeur. Roads were mere paths which turned to streams when torrents of rain broke loose; dingy shops darkened by awnings of leaves, selling cotton goods and hardware, lined the narrow, ill-paved streets; sudden and violent thunderstorms made the plaster fall off walls; the squalor made skin diseases and sores commonplace; naked slaves in a 'dreadful state of misery and destitution' were disembarked at the Customs House, and sold as if 'they were cattle', to remorseless buyers. At least, that's what a young Glasgow traveller reported in the *Glasgow Herald*, in 1865, the same year Caetano do Rosario de Souza opened a store on the island.

The arrival of C. R. de Souza marks the beginning of a Goan presence in Zanzibar. But there were Goans living there prior to that; the Spiritan Vicar Apostolic Raoul de Courmont, in 1860, counted 'seven or eight' Catholics on the island 'who had come from Goa'. Three decades later, he was told by 'trustworthy sources' that the Goans 'are coming here especially because they have the assurance of finding here both priests and a Catholic mission'.

Catholic piety aside, just who were these handful of Goans that the vicar had prayed with and what were they doing in Zanzibar? Were they traders who had sailed from nearby Mozambique, then part

Landing beach, Zanzibar, c.1890-1900.
In the distance is the British ship Nerbudda. Goans working on board British ships would have been part of the floating population of mid-nineteenth century Zanzibar. Nearby was the Smith Mackenzie & Co. office, agents for British India ships.

Chaiton D'Almeida Born c.1852 in Zanzibar. Work history as per the records of the Royal Navy Registers of Seamen's Services.

of Portuguese East Africa or could there be some other possibility?

The British Royal Navy may well provide us with a clue. In 1878, they had on their muster roll, a 'man of colour' and 'very good conduct', one Chaiton D'Almeida, who for the next seventeen years worked as ship's cook. (Chaiton is a corruption of the Goan name Caetan). His date of birth is given as 1852; his place of birth as Zanzibar. How did Chaiton come to be born in Zanzibar? Almost certainly, Chaiton would have been of biracial Goan and African stock, because there were no Goan women in Zanzibar at the time.

Chaiton's choice of occupations - and indeed they were two separate occupations - that of a *tarvotti* (seafarer) and a cook, is interesting. Traditional occupations were inherited. It is likely that his father had arrived in Zanzibar engaged on board a ship and it was not unusual for *tarvottis* to take up employment or trading on land intermittently and then return to the sea after a few years. It was this occupation -seafaring - which would open up a new migratory life for Goans, as they docked in alien ports.

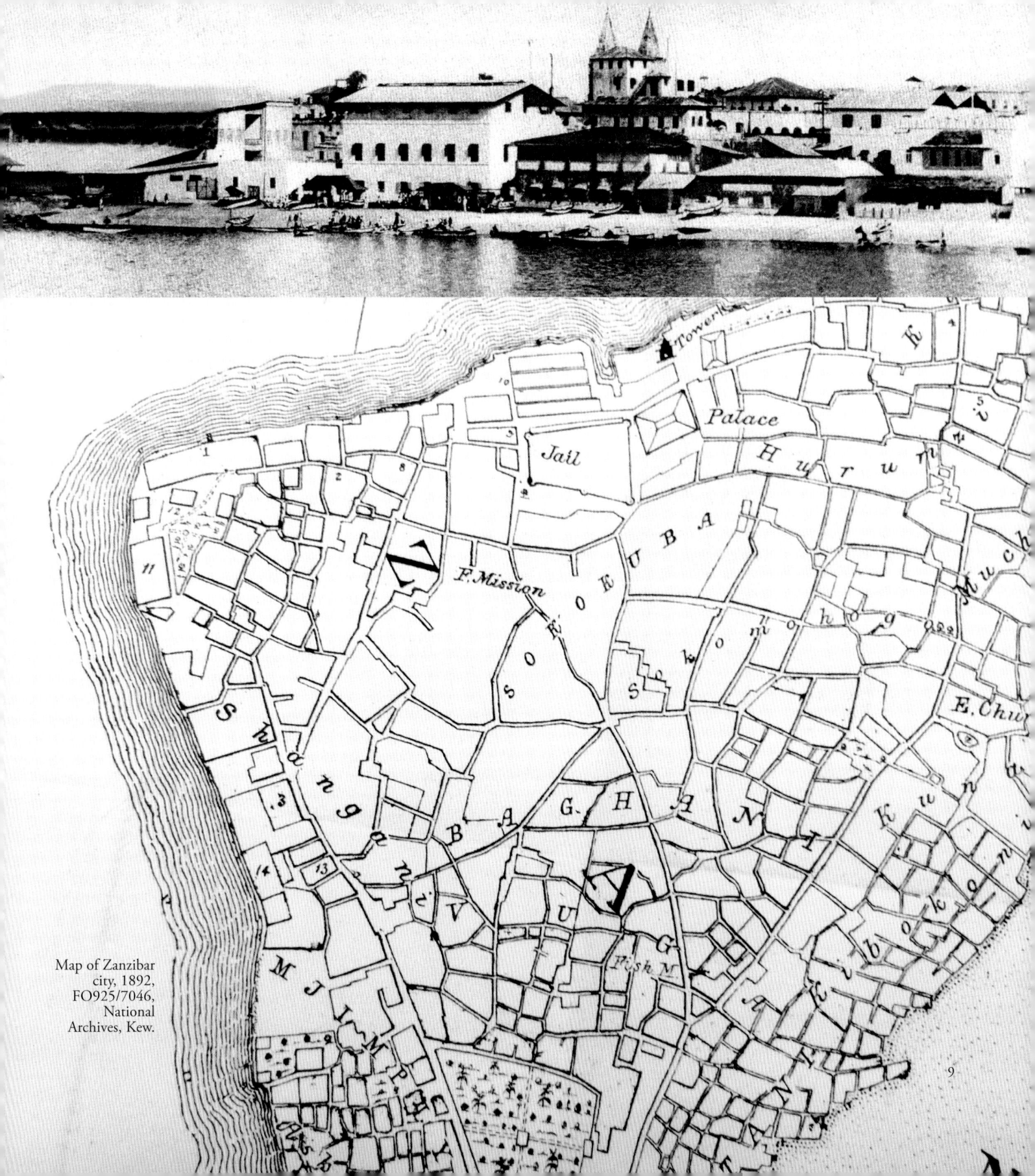

Map of Zanzibar city, 1892, FO925/7046, National Archives, Kew.

Portuguese Street, Zanzibar, c.1880-1890. Along this street, the earliest Goan traders arriving in Zanzibar set up shop supplying flour, bread, meat and vegetables to ships docked nearby. The sign-board for Dr F. P. Paixoa de Noronha's dispensary can be seen in the centre and to the left is Peter Paulo de Souza's general provision store. Other Goan traders to have started out on Portuguese Street include C. R. de Souza, L. M. de Souza, and Sequeira, Souza & Co.

'PORTUGUESE STREET': THE ARRIVAL OF GOAN TRADERS

A 1892 map of Zanzibar shows a small protrusion of land on the westerly shore providing a natural harbour and front for a number of consulates, the Sultan's palace, the Customs House, and a telegraph and post office. Those early Goans, who had arrived in the second half of the 19th century, found themselves living cheek-by-jowl in the labyrinthine alleyways along Portuguese Street. From the front-end of their dwellings, they operated provision stores, bakeries, butcheries, laundries, grog-shops and tailoring outlets, spurred on by the business they secured from the 'large fleet of dhows and several European merchant ships' anchored in the nearby harbour. As with Cape Town, Zanzibar grew on a port economy of refuelling, provisioning and entertaining ship crews.

The close relationship between Goans working on board ships and their compatriots on land would have played a crucial role in securing naval contracts. Ship stewards and cooks were entrusted with food provisioning, and while on shore leave, they were known to frequent Goan-run portside taverns. Profitable alliances between crew and tavern-owner would have formed over home-cooked meals and alcohol-fuelled bonhomie. The taverns were not the only meeting place though; ship crews, once docked, were invited to friendly matches of football - island residents versus the floating population of sailors. Even the Portuguese vice-consul played his part by hosting naval officers, possibly to cement these sea-land relationships.

By 1875, the British consulate estimated there to be fifty-nine Goans on the island, a modest estimate which six years later had ballooned to 174 odd, who appeared as signatories on an open letter of appreciation addressed to Consul-General Sir John Kirk. Some of this growth was an outflow from neighbouring Portuguese East Africa. Caetano Felicio de Souza of Sequeira, Souza & Co, for instance, had left his partners in Mozambique's ailing Porto Amelia, to trade independently in Zanzibar. These were family-run businesses whose arterial spread grew when family from Goa joined them, and after a few years splintered from the main holding. Men convinced siblings, cousins and nephews to join them in Africa. Marriages were sealed if the potential for a hard-working brother-in-law existed.

Advertisement for John Peter de Souza's Bakery & Butchery, *Zanzibar Gazette*, 9 February, 1898.

> **John Peter de Souza**
> ZANZIBAR.
>
> **BAKERY & BUTCHERY**
>
> Established 1867
>
> **NAVAL CONTRACTOR,**
> PRESERVED & FRESH PROVISIONS
> SUPPLIER TO SHIPS OF ALL NATIONS,
> WINE & SPIRIT DEALER:
> *CIVIL & NAVAL TAILOR.*
> OUTFITTER AND GENERAL MERCHANT
> *Best Testimonials secured.*
> All orders promptly executed and at moderate prices.
> Fresh stores of provisions, Flour always on hand.
> HEAD ESTABLISHMENT......Portuguese Street
> BRANCHES............Pangani, & Tanga.

Among the early arrivals was John Peter de Souza, who in 1867 opened a small bakery and butchery promising 'flour always on hand'. Goan renown for quality bread and confectionery aided in this fiercely competitive market. Even Domingos Baptista Pereira who arrived in 1869, and later enjoyed great success and affluence, started out with a modest bakery and butchery. Pereira had obviously earned his stripes. One public notice of recognition put in the papers by Commander E. Incoronata praised the efficiency with which Pereira had executed the contract to supply 'fresh beef and bread' to the royal ship while docked.

Ships' ledgers show just how symbiotic the relationship between Europe's sea empires and Goans was, with entries detailing money owed to traders. Doctors too were essential to the sea-land network; Dr Paixao de Noronha, for example, was a regular supplier of muriatic acid which, at the time, was stocked by ships as a sterilising agent. To meet the housing demand of this burgeoning male migration, landlords such as Joaquim Freitas took over boarding houses, providing 'rooms alone or with food' at moderate charges.

Despite the meteoric rise to prominence of a few Goan traders - C. R. de Souza, L. M. de Souza, Souza Junior & Dias, D. B. Pereira and his son-in-law Pedro Francisco de Souza - others had only middling success or faced destitution with changing business conditions. Goan 'grog shops in swarms' lined the streets, distributing alcohol much to the irritation of British retail interests; their livelihoods dependent on the caprices of Protestant morality. Policing of alcohol sale resulted in an Anglo-Portuguese agreement restricting the number of Goan liquor shops to just thirty. But it was the Brussels Conference Act of 1890, seeking to regulate import and distribution of alcohol that would deal the cruellest blow, forcing small-time traders to contemplate either returning to Goa or moving to the German colony of Tanganyika.

'UNIVERSAL PROVIDER': C. R. DE SOUZA

During his time in Zanzibar, C. R de Souza became embroiled in at least two controversial and litigious battles; one with French missionaries over a land dispute, and the other with his former manager Pedro Francisco de Souza over money owed. But there is little doubt that Souza, a renowned philanthropist, was considered the pioneer and patriarch of the Goan community in Zanzibar.

Souza grew up in close proximity to the sea. The village of Velsao, where he was born on 7 February, 1839, to Joao Francisco and Eulalia Godinho, is fronted by a beach. Of the family, little is known except that they were landowners, and judging by their marriage alliances, they must have been a family of some standing, for in Goa, no amount of wealth accumulation could overcome caste barriers. In later years, Souza would greatly enhance the family reputation by becoming a benefactor of several chapels including Our Lady of Lourdes in Betalbatim and St. Anthony's Chapel in Deussua. Likely, the family was politically opinionated; quite apart from Souza publicly voicing his displeasure at the 1890 Margao Church square massacre, a later marriage alliance bound the Souza family with the Loyola-Furtados, the most volatile name in Goan politics prior to liberation.

A surviving photograph of Souza reveals a large man wearing a lengthened beard and a number of medals pinned onto an expansive chest. As a young man Souza showed a keen interest in merchant shipping and by his mid-twenties he had set sail for Africa. Once there, he shrewdly imported the concept of a store as a communal space, of the kind that exist on the periphery of every Goan church square. Fairly quickly, he established himself as vital to the retail trade of the island. His reputation as 'universal provider' was not worn lightly.

Quite confident of his ability to deliver, he advertised his store as carrying 'every description of goods used by Europeans'. Anyone stocking up to go on a mainland expedition or join the caravan trail would stop by at his store. Bishop Hannington frequented the store, perhaps buying one of the *Letts* diaries which Souza kept in stock, before Hannington's ill-fated expedition into Uganda, where he and his Goan cook Pinto were grotesquely murdered. In just fifteen years, Sultan Sayyid Barghash awarded him a 'diploma of honour with a gold medal' for enterprise. Further recognition came in 1892, when he was

Right
Roldao Souza with wife Jovita, c.1910. Upon Souza's death, the business was taken over by his two sons Eliseu and Roldao.

Far right
C. R. de Souza store, Main Road, Zanzibar, c.1902. Souza advertised his store as carrying 'every description of goods used by Europeans'. Among the things sold were wines, cutlery, stationery, medicines, perfumes, rifles, drapery, and boots & shoes. In 1902, the brothers opened a branch on Main Road and in 1906, a branch in Mombasa.

honoured once again by Sayyid Ali bin Sayyid.

Souza's moniker of 'Big de Souza', possibly had as much to do with his large girth as it had with his unparalleled prestige amongst Goans. Souza became the father figure for destitute Goans in Zanzibar; he enabled the migration of countless Goans by employing them in his establishment, and encouraging them whenever possible to start out on their own. One such protégé was Souza Junior & Dias, started in 1890 by Felix Dias and Manuelino de Souza. They took huge risks and gambled on diversifying quickly into Dar es Salaam, Bagamoyo, Tanga and Kilwa. Manuelino died shortly afterwards and Reginaldo de Souza, his brother, took his place. In time, they would grow into a trading, ship chandling and real estate empire.

Even more admirable, and in keeping with the Christian ethos of an educated citizenry, Souza paid for the education of some of his employees' children. Never appointed to any official position, he nonetheless was the spokesperson for the Goan community prior to a consul being appointed by Portugal. In 1894, Portugal, in recognition of his philanthropic and leadership role, decorated him with the *Ordem de Cristo*.

With the demise of Souza in 1900, the C. R. de Souza store, for a while, was administered by his wife Roza Marianne Martine with the assistance of a lawyer until the sons, Eliseu and Roldao took over. In 1902, they opened a branch on Main Street, trading under the name the English Stores. They would only re-emerge as serious contenders for retail excellence when in 1906 they opened a branch in Mombasa.

Caetano R. de Souza, c.1895.
In 1865, Souza opened the C. R. de Souza store in Zanzibar. Just fifteen years later, Sultan Sayyid Barghash awarded him a 'diploma of honour with a gold medal' for enterprise. A renowned philanthropist, Souza is considered to be the patriarch of Goan migration into British East Africa.

Sultan's Military band, c.1890.
The band was led by a succession of Goan bandmasters. In 1890, the bandmaster was Diogo Sant-Anna de Souza.

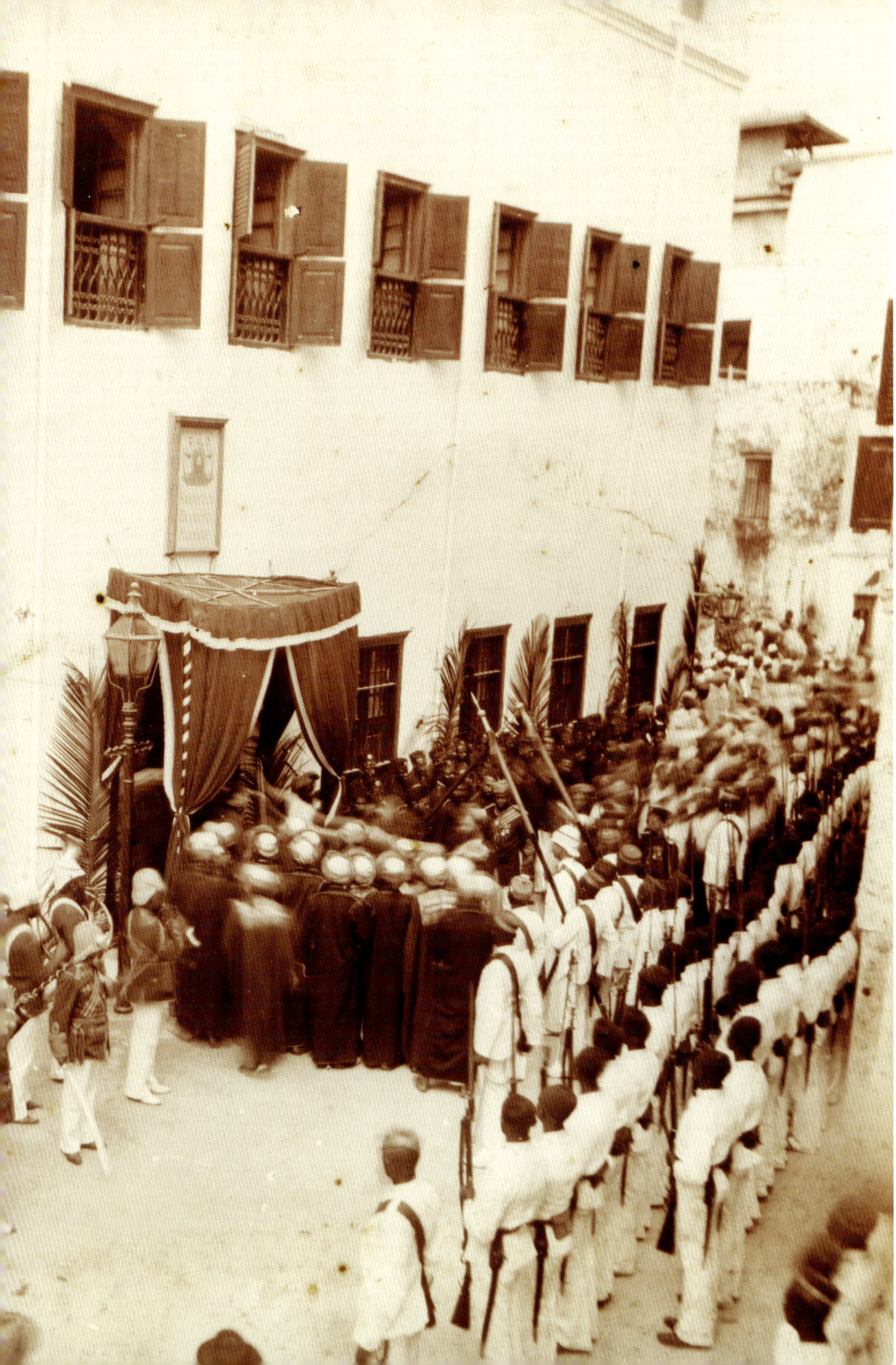

'THE JOLLY FRIVOLITY BOYS': THE SULTAN'S GOAN BAND

The princeling Sayid Barghash-bin-Sayid had been exiled by the British to Bombay, where he led not-too-shabby a life for two years on an allowance of 12,000 rupees. After his return in 1861, and particularly after he assumed power a near-decade later, Goans begin to appear as part of the palace's musical retinue. Starting from 1876, the forty-five year old Diogo Sant-Anna de Souza held 'one of the most prominent posts' in Zanzibar - that of bandmaster. He retired in 1897 and died the same year from chest complications. Barghash might have known Sant-Anna as an aspiring musician, during his time in Bombay. At any rate, Barghash would have been familiar with Goan musicians who found ready employment in the royal courts of India. Soon, the band comprised almost entirely of Goans including Sant-Anna's son and son-in-law, and was known on the island as the 'Sultan's Goanese band'.[1]

Upon retirement, Sant-Anna's place was taken by Camillo A. Saldanha as first bandmaster and Isaac de Souza-Khot as second bandmaster, both of whom had joined about the same time as Sant-Anna. Camillo and Isaac became minor celebrities. Together they organised weekly musical programmes of waltzes and polkas, and held concerts every Wednesday evening at the Victoria Gardens. Zanzibar slowly came alive; their concerts became the not-to-be-missed event of the week attended by large crowds.

When Camillo retired in 1900, Isaac took over as first bandmaster and propelled the reputation of the band to even greater heights. Sporting an enviable Kaiser moustache, the uniquely gifted virtuoso composed his own music including a waltz entitled *Binti Unguja*. This was hardly surprising, for Isaac the son of Rosario de Souza-Khot from the Goan village of Saligao, came from a family of prodigiously talented musicians. Another of the Khot siblings, Manuel de Souza-Khot, was also a bandmaster at a royal court. Khot is a Konkan tittle-surname of revenue collecting farming families and was likely retained after converting to Catholicism.

With Isaac's expanded repertoire, the band played jaunty sessions every Saturday evening between 5 p.m and 6 p.m, at the Mnazi Moja Club. Isaac prepared weekly musical programmes to be played

---
[1] The term Goanese may be offensive to some but it has been retained within quotes to accurately reflect the terminology of the period.

Above
Military medals awarded to Isaac de Souza Khot, First Bandmaster (1900-1906) of the Sultan's Military band.

Above right
The Band Programme, *Zanzibar Gazette*, 16 March, 1898.

at Victoria Gardens, which included marches such the *'The Jolly Frivolity Boys'* by composer Hume and sophisticated waltzes by Strauss. Often, the band was loaned by the Sultan to play for ceremonial occasions in Mombasa. Isaac left the Sultan's employ in 1906 with a token gift of Rs 722, raised at a benefit show in his honour. During his tenure, he had been paid a paltry sum of Rs 150 per month, the equivalent of a government clerk's salary, but he was held in high regard. The British Consul-General Basil Cave took up the matter of his pension with Foreign Secretary Sir Edward Grey, and an annual sum of Rs 660 was agreed upon. Souza's replacement, Jayme Candido de Campos, hired from Portugal, continued the grand tradition of the band, making his debut with the Brazilian polka *Maxixe*. But the reign of Goans as first bandmasters had come to an end.

'AMID THE FIRING OF SALUTES': BRITISH PROTECTORATE

Zanzibar's strategic location as 'the central market for very many smaller ports situated on the adjacent mainland' made it integral to Britain's twin aspirations of 'profit and Protestantism'.

Having been under the shadowy influence of Britain since consular relations were established in 1841, Zanzibar inevitably became a full-fledged British protectorate in 1890. 'No great ceremony marked the occasion'; the flags of Britain and Zanzibar were hoisted 'amid the firing of salutes'. The calm in the changing of guard reflected the extent to which Britain had already usurped power in the region over some decades. The Sultan, reduced to a figurehead with an annual privy purse of Rs 300,000, relinquished his hold over government departments which British officials charged were in chaos. The solution: to immediately create various departments 'placed under English officials'. The Welshman, General William Lloyd Mathews was appointed first minister of Zanzibar and assigned, with 'great hopes', for the purpose of reconstituting and remodelling the Sultan's government.

Goans working for the Sultan found themselves in the employ of the British administration. The prestige they enjoyed previously might have been eclipsed, and some nudged into an early retirement, but most Goans retained their positions, even up to inspector and superintendent level. If anything, their numbers increased in the following decades as they moved in, to fill low to mid-level administrative jobs. In the process, the Goans of Zanzibar underwent another transformation; that of becoming steadily Anglicised and loyal to the British.

'MASTER OF THE HORSE': GOAN DOCTORS

The explorer Dr David Livingstone's March 1866 journal entry left little to the imagination. 'The stench', he wrote, 'from a mile and a half to two miles of exposed sea beach, which is the general depository of the filth of the town, is quite horrible. At night it is so gross or crass one might cut out a slice and manure a garden with it: it might be called Stinkibar rather than Zanzibar. No one can enjoy good health here'. Explorer Richard Burton, ten years earlier, had listed diseases prevalent on the island: dysentery, yellow fever, malaria, cholera and inflammation. Other travellers left their own impressions. Donald Mackenzie, three decades after Livingstone's visit, still thought the streets to be 'particularly dirty', and believed the damp heat and nearby swamp brought on fevers.

Given this state of affairs, it was only natural for Zanzibar's ruling elite to be rather fond of their attending physicians. Around 1870, Dr Francisco Piedade Paixao de Noronha set up his medical practice on the island. Almost certainly, he was a palace physician, and played an important role in the affairs of the Goan community. When in 1881, the Goan residents of Zanzibar sent an open letter to the British Consul-General Kirk, the signatories featured in order of prominence had Noronha listed second only to C. R. de Souza.

Doctors invariably had a much wider role in the Sultan's palace than just tending to the sick. They were confidantes and at times part of the royal entourage. Colonial administrator Harry Johnston, in 1885, referred to 'wily Goanese' acting as intermediaries between the Sultan and European officials. In all probability, it was these multilingual doctors with fluency in Portuguese, English and French and some knowledge of local languages who would have been called upon to facilitate conversation with foreign dignitaries.[1] Zanzibar would be served by other noteworthy Goan doctors; of those, one who would rise to unparalleled prominence was Dr Luis Antonio de Andrade, known in the bustling port as Master of the Horse.

Andrade was born in 1865, in Damao, a Portuguese colonial enclave on the western coast of India. His twice-married grandfather and namesake from Viseu, Portugal, had emigrated to Damao. José

---

[1] The official interpreter at the Arabic court, Lewis Luke Antoni might also have had a Goan affiliation. He was married to Louise Marie de Souza and either he or his wife had family in Bombay. A later appointed Goan interpreter at the Judicial department was Francis Phillip hired in 1905.

António, Andrade's father, might have been a *decendente*[2] but his mother Rosa Moniz could trace her family roots to the landed gentry of Benaulim in Goa. Educated in Bombay and Lisbon, Andrade at twenty-four set sail for Zanzibar. Soon, he assumed the post of medical assistant to Sultan Sayyid Ali Bin Sayid and veterinary surgeon to the government.

By 1892, he was in the employ of the British protectorate government. Between 1904 and 1906, Andrade's overarching powers extended far beyond that of tending to the sick. He was put in charge of the crown lands department and then promoted to collector of Inland Revenue while simultaneously holding the portfolio of (acting) director of agriculture. Shortly thereafter, he became town collector, being paid a salary of £520 per annum. Eventually, he was appointed district commissioner of Zanzibar.

A glimpse into Andrade's everyday life can be had from a letter he wrote in 1906 to the British official General Raikes, protesting against his office being shifted: 'Being as it is now under my house I have not only the advantage of having the constant services of a clerk who sleeps on the premises, but I am always about and see what is going on. The income of the markets comes to the office at 3 p.m and 6.30 p.m. All the pice have to be counted, bundled and kept ready to be sent to the treasury… at all times of the day and often at nights, cattle have to be examined for the ships or for slaughtering purposes'.

Andrade's racial identification is hard to discern. Possibly, he never felt conflicted enough to compartmentalise his identity. He was every bit entrenched in European society as a member of European clubs and a Fellow of the Royal Geographical Society of Lisbon. But he was an intrinsic part of the Goan community and an unwavering supporter of Goan causes. He considered Portugal his home but he visited India as well. As an employee of the protectorate, the British accepted him as sufficiently European to rise to the position of district commissioner. Photographed on occasion wearing an African-styled *fez*, he was decorated with several honours including the Brilliant Star of Zanzibar by the Sultan, and Chevalier of the Order of the Immaculate Conception by Portugal.[3] Every bit the imperial man, Andrade's ability to straddle different cultures and form long-standing relationships epitomise the grace and cultural dexterity of an early transnational.

---

[2] Descendente, progeny of white Portuguese settlers in Asia.
[3] Andrade was decorated with third class of the Order of Hamoudieh, second class of the Order of El Aliyah, second class Brilliant Star of Zanzibar, Chevalier of the Order of the Immaculate Conception (Portugal) and Grand Commander of the Military Order of Christ.

On board the *H. H. S Cupid.* Sultan of Zanzibar and British officials, c.1912. Dr Luis A. Andrade (standing second left, in a white suit).

'VIEWS AND PICTORIAL POSTCARDS': GOAN PHOTOGRAPHERS

By the turn of the century, A. C. Gomes enjoyed a certain celebrityhood in East Africa. In March 1914, no less than the Colonial Office Visual Instruction Committee, responsible for publications about Britain's colonies, requested Gomes permission to reproduce his pictures as book illustrations and lantern slides. Gomes obliged, provided they were duly attributed. It was not the first time, the merit of his work had been publicly acknowledged; in 1906 the Zanzibar Committee for the Irish International Exhibition, to be held in Dublin the following year, had commissioned him to make a 'series of studies illustrative of the clove industry', in Fufuni - the first study of its kind.

In all likelihood, the slightly built, bespectacled A. C. Gomes was the earliest photographer to open a studio in Zanzibar, sometime between 1868 and 1869. He had relocated from Aden, where he had been appointed government photographer. Gomes ran a studio on Main Road opposite the General Post Office, later with the assistance of his son P. F. Gomes.

J. B. Coutinho who would gain recognition in his own right, initially partnered with A. C. Gomes but confident of success, he dissolved the arrangement in July 1897, and along with his brother Felix set up shop as the Coutinho Brothers - photographers and rubber stampmakers. Success came fairly quickly; the following year the Coutinhos were appointed photographers to the Sultan and added 'several interesting photos of Zanzibar' to their collection. Business was thriving. In 1900, they moved to a larger studio adjoining Mory Printing Press, where apart from views of Zanzibar, they sold Dutch cigars in their busy showroom always crowded with people.

Emboldened by the potential of the tourist trade, Andrew Richard Pereira de Lord from Salvador do Mundo in Goa, also opened a studio. Photography was a family business; Pereira's father Joseph Joaquim Pereira ran a studio in Margao, Goa, and his brother Dominic carried on the family business in Jubbulpore, Madhya Pradesh. The popularity of the medium with the government and royal patrons provided a boost to photographers in India enabling them to turn their skill into an art form.

By 1906, Pereira had a much sought-after studio on Corner Lane, selling 'views and pictorial

Andrew Richard Pereira de Lord.

Letter from A. C. Gomes, 26 March, 1914. Leasing reproduction rights of his photographs to the Colonial Office Visual Instruction Committee.

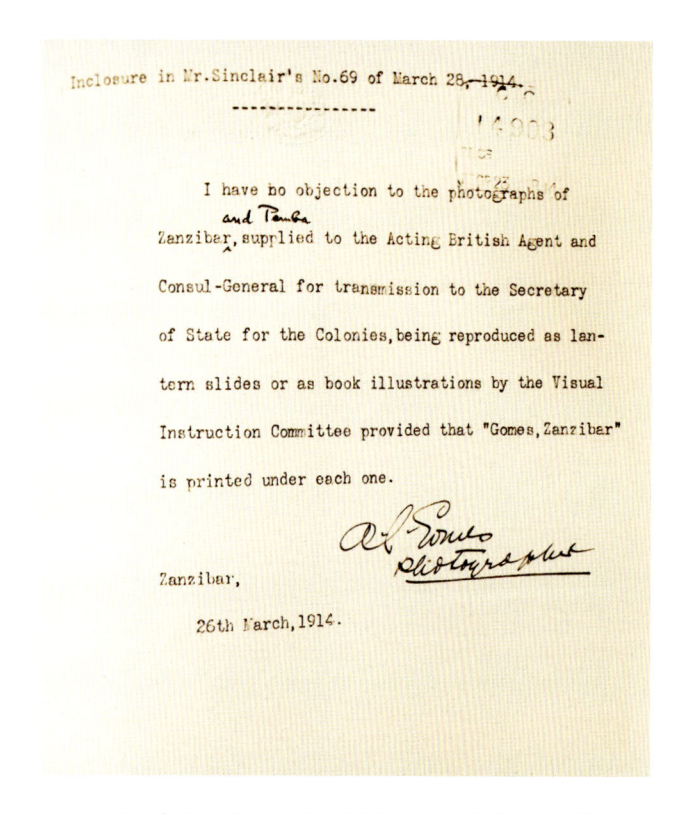

> Inclosure in Mr.Sinclair's No.69 of March 28, 1914.
>
> I have no objection to the photographs of and Pemba Zanzibar, supplied to the Acting British Agent and Consul-General for transmission to the Secretary of State for the Colonies, being reproduced as lantern slides or as book illustrations by the Visual Instruction Committee provided that "Gomes, Zanzibar" is printed under each one.
>
> *A. C. Gomes, photographer*
>
> Zanzibar,
> 26th March, 1914.

postcards of Zanzibar and neighbourhood'. Some of his surviving work shows a profound love of the subject matter: the flora and fauna of Zanzibar, African women, and idle boats lying along a forlorn coast. The business then added on watch, clock and typewriter repairs. Caetano Joseph Pereira, a younger brother, partnered with Andrew for a while before joining the civil service.

From Zanzibar, photographers opened branches in Mombasa, Nairobi and other townships across East Africa. Domingos Vincente Figueira known popularly as D. V. Figueira, son of Aleixo Figueira and Deudita Paulina de Sa from Figueira *vaddo* (district) in Guirim, Goa, operated The Studio on Main Street, Mombasa.

These Goan photographers relied heavily on the patronage of British officials but primarily they were commercial artists who made a living selling postcards to tourists. With advances in photography, they expanded their subject matter and ventured out of their studios to take on 'outdoor work'. In this respect, they were documenting people, events, landscape and their inherent interlocking relationships. They projected a 'third eye' different from that of colonial and indigenous perspectives, and created a visual narrative whose relevance survives to this day.

The Pereira de Lord Photo Studio on the Main Road. They also operated a studio and workshop on Corner Lane.

DE LORD'S PHOTO STORES
AND CITY SALES.
DEVELOPING
PRINTING
ENLARGING ETC.
H.H.M. DE SILVA
MILK

Joaosinho Simao Figueira, manager of the *Zanzibar Gazette* from 1893 until he retired in 1916.

'RELATIONS WITH EVERYONE': GOAN NEWSMEN

An entity involved with the shaping of public opinion could hardly have been left alone to lead an independent existence. One such entity was the *Gazette*, subsumed by the British administration as soon as Zanzibar became a protectorate. Surprising then, that the British retained as its manager, a Goan, Joaosinho Simao Figueira.

Born in the village of Guirim in north Goa to Diogo Francisco and Anna Sebastiana, family lore informs that Figueira was the first Goan to leave for Africa from the Figueira *vaddo*. The family's occupation on death certificates is noted as *'proprietarios'* (landed gentry).

The *Gazette for Zanzibar & East Africa* had been launched in February 1892 by the London-based merchant house Forwood Bros. & Co. Exactly how Figueira came to be recruited by the Forwood Bros. is not known but he would have been no more than in his twenties when he joined them in December 1892. The following year, he took over as manager of the *Gazette* from F. W. Campin. The ownership passed to the government in 1894, becoming the official organ for disseminating information about regulations, trade reports, shipping schedules and general affairs. From then on, until he retired in 1916, the even-tempered Figueira managed the *Gazette's* operations and the task of maintaining continuity, and coordinating with various departments fell to him. This prompted, the editor, Rivers-Smith to commend 'the tact' shown in his 'relations with everyone'. Of his Bombay-recruited staff members, at least six were Goan.

It is difficult to discern just how much impact Figueira had on the editorial content of the publication; most of the submissions came from residents or visitors to the island. And Figueira was overseen by a British official, either a health officer or director of education, who in his spare time would be lumbered with editorial responsibilities. What is obvious though, is that during Figueira's tenure, a disproportionately high number of articles relating to Goan personalities appeared on the *Gazette's* pages and it is hard to discount his hand in those stories. Substantial revenues of the *Gazette* emerged from the full-length page advertisements taken out by Goan merchants such C. R. de Souza and Luis Manuel de Souza. Clearly, it was this robust advertising patronage which also compelled the newspaper to carry stories

Joaosinho Simao Figueira possibly with other printing press staff. His team in 1913, included Alexander A. Albuquerque as proof-reader; Augustine Francis Pinto, Augustus Fernandes, Mariano Caetano de Souza, Hasham Alarakhia, Sultan Kutub and Thani bin Gathei as compositors; John Christidas and Seif bin Khalfan as pressmen.

about Goans. The close relationships Figueira enjoyed within the community with the likes of Dr M. F. de Albuquerque, mentioned in a diary he kept, and Luis Manuel de Souza his father-in-law, could only have had a productive effect on the revenue and submissions to the *Gazette*.

When ill-health prompted Figueira's retirement after twenty-four years of service, he summed up his contribution as having spanned and survived seven editors, several acting editors, five sultans, two forcible seizures of the palace and one bombardment. During that time, his name had been transmuted on official documents to John Simon. The unusually high annual salary for an Asian of Rs 3,900 near the time of retirement and subsequently his annual pension of £99, reflected the extent to which the British establishment had come to rely on Figueira. His replacement was Joseph Thomas Riches.

Shortly after retirement, Figueira moved to Nairobi presumably to spend time with his wife Preciosa Liberata's family. While there, he entered into partnership with Antonio Caetano de Souza, trading as general merchants and caterers under the auspices of the East Africa Store, owned by the late L. M. de Souza. In November 1917, the short-lived partnership between Antonio Souza and Figueira was dissolved, and Figueira returned to Goa where he died in 1919.

'TRES GRANDE DISTINCTION': GOAN DIPLOMATS

Portugal's slumbering imperial ambitions in Africa were at times aided by indigenous Goans. Too enfeebled to venture into the interior, Portugal's coastal garrisons maintained control over Mozambique. Nonetheless, Portugal retained its sovereignty in the interior well beyond Mozambique's porous borders and into the Zambezi valley by bequeathing *prazos* (crown estates) to Goans. These slave-trading Goan *prazeiros* professed allegiance to Portugal but for all purposes were autonomous feudatories. Some were absentee landlords, governing from elsewhere, often a home in Goa; others were hands-on overlords, dreaded for their despotic ruthlessness in exacting hard labour and extorting revenues from the slave-trade.

When the *prazos* eventually fell into decline by the 19th century, Goans still played a role in sustaining the Iberian empire. The adventurer Daniel Rankin found, in 1890, at Ibo, Angoche and Chilwan, 'a few sickly, badly-drilled garrisons commanded by Goanese'. That the Goans looked sickly was Rankin's euphemism for how weak a threat Portugal posed, were Britain to exert her expansionist aspirations in the Zambezi and Shire valley, which it had every intention of doing.

When Portugal was not using Goans as overlords, troops and priests in the service of empire or relying on the solitary Goan trader to venture into the hinterland, it looked to them for diplomatic and consular support in British controlled East Africa. The chosen man, almost always a prominent doctor or on a rare occasion a businessman, would fly the Portuguese flag at full mast outside his surgery or home. These men were what the Portuguese called *assimilados*; except for their skin colour, they were in every respect bourgeois, metropolitan Portuguese who profoundly believed in the glory of empire. The designated title was usually 'vice-consul of the Portuguese nation' (or in a lesser capacity consular agent) in whatever territory they were appointed. The task of this role was to engender a sense of nationhood; a separateness from other subjects and a continued enculturation. These Goan diplomats proved to be enormously effectively. They remained enduringly loyal to Portugal while pledging fealty to the British Crown and saw no contradiction in this twinning of nationalist sympathies.

In 1884, Portugal appointed their flag-bearing explorer Serpa Pinto as consul-general in Zanzibar.

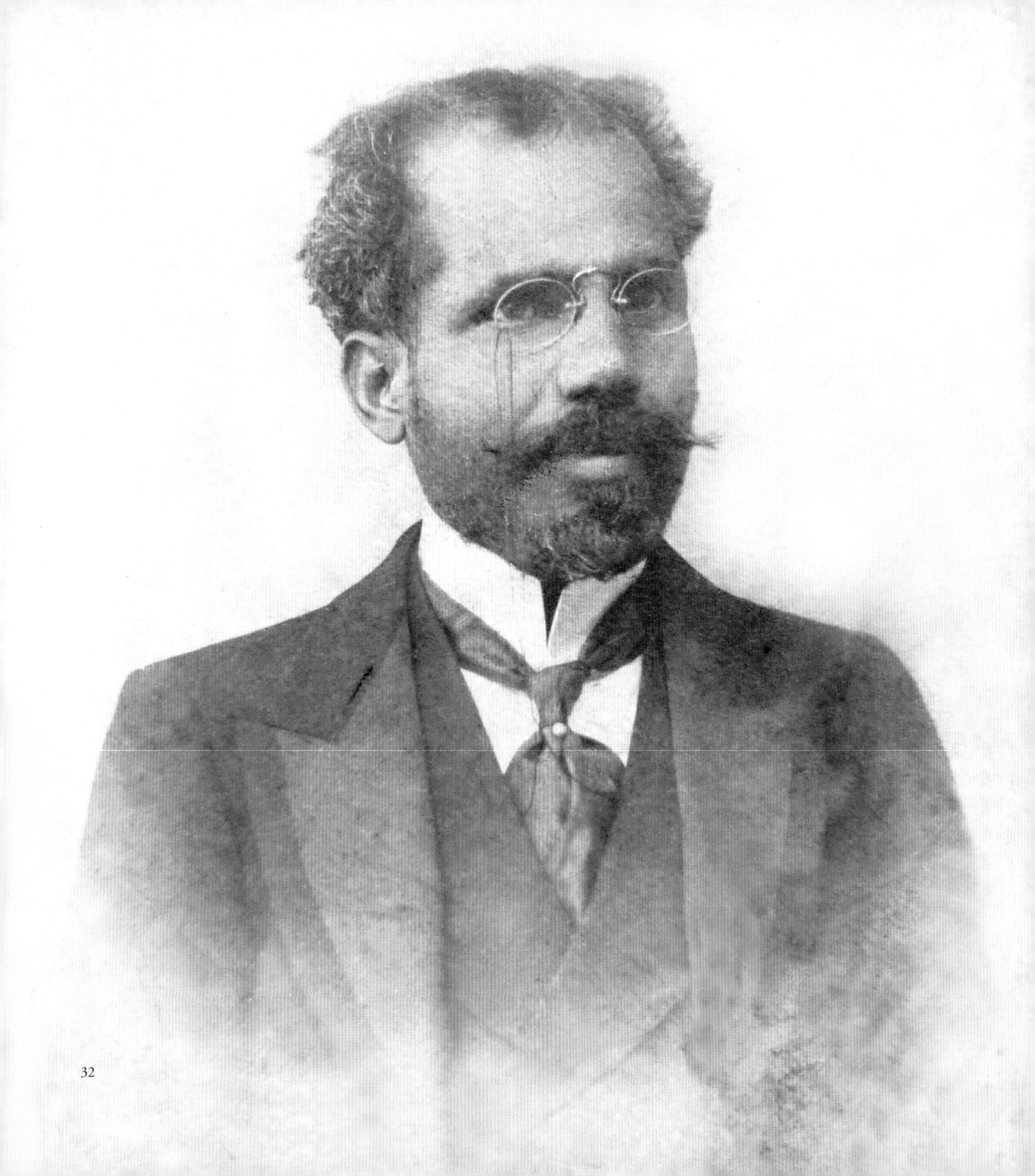

Barely had he assumed the title, he was off on another expedition and the actual task of maintaining consular responsibilities fell to Dr Augusto Braz de Souza, appointed vice-consul in 1885.

Like many aspiring young men born to privilege and having the means to acquire a higher education, Braz had studied medicine. The establishment of the Escola Médico-Cirúrgica de (Nova) Goa in 1842, the first of its kind in Asia, proved to be a turning point in colonial history. It opened up a new career path for Goan men and produced the archetypal 'soldier-doctor'. Nor had the British been idle. From 1824, there were medical training institutions in Calcutta with the aim of providing assistant surgeons, apothecaries and dressers for the army. When Grant Medical College opened in Bombay in November 1845, men such as Braz who graduated there, were enthusiastically absorbed into the British-India army.

In 1881, on the cusp of his thirtieth birthday, urged by his brother Casmiro de Souza, Braz arrived in Zanzibar. The training Braz had as assistant physician at the European military hospital in Colaba, Bombay, would stand him in good stead. By 1891, the Sultan Sayyid bin Ali had decorated him with the Order of the Brilliant Star of Zanzibar. In 1892, he was accorded the title of Portuguese consul.

As the century came to a close, the house of Braz fell from grace. In 1894, an imbroglio with French missionaries led to his humiliating dismissal as consul-general. An effete Portuguese government, keen to save diplomatic face, recalled him from office and instructed Captain Vianno Basto to restore to the missionaries the contested lands and funds. Braz had other problems plaguing him. Creditors knocked at his door. A law suit filed, in 1898, by Sayyid Abdallah bin Mahmoud and Sayyid Hamed bin Mahmoud compelled Braz to offer his dispensary and home as guarantee. He died soon after, aged just fifty, leaving his widow Guilheimina Quitera Viegas to administer his estate.

Braz's departure from the diplomatic scene made way for another Goan who would assume the role with much more vigour. In the summer of 1898, the twenty-nine year old Dr Manuel Francisco de Albuquerque arrived in Zanzibar by a French mail steamer.

It would appear that the Goan community was being prepared for Dr Albuquerque. An announcement in the *Zanzibar Gazette*, giving his resume, preceded his arrival. His father Angelo Maria d'Albuquerque was a long-time resident of the island in the employ of Smith Mackenzie & Co, and quite prominent, as a contemporary of C. R. de Souza, in Goan affairs.

Upon graduating from Grant Medical College in 1896, Albuquerque had left for Edinburgh where he passed his final L.R.C.P (medical graduation), obtained his MD *'avec tres grande distinction'* in Brussels, and trained for a short while in Paris. Once in Zanzibar, he was appointed palace physician and ran a successful practice at Surgical Hall on Main Road, which served as his surgery, pharmacy and living quarters. He opened two branches and employed four clerks, selling English, French and American specialities, tabloids, Mere sanitary towels for women and optical lenses. In an early public act of

Dr M. F. de Albuquerque, c.1898.

Surgical Hall, c.1905. Where Dr M. F. de Albuquerque practiced and resided.

philanthropy, Albuquerque made a substantial donation to the Famine Relief Fund of 1899.

Albuquerque immediately assumed the leadership role for which he was clearly suited. An opportune moment for just such leadership presented itself in May 1900, with the arrival of the much-decorated Colonel Joaquim José Machado enroute to Mozambique. At the invitation of Albuquerque, a delegation of Goans met the former governor of Goa, at the Africa Hotel. The Goans arrived bearing gifts; they presented Machado with a pair of ebony elephant-shaped heads and a gold bracelet set with diamonds and rubies. Impressed by their apparent prosperity, Machado fussed that, 'the activity of the sons of Goa, which is so evidently manifest in foreign countries will yet one day be employed in their own country'.

It is possible Albuquerque had already developed a relationship with the Portuguese foreign ministry while in Europe. A surviving photograph of a youngish looking Albuquerque, has Calcada do Duque, 25 Lisboa as the studio address, so presumably, he had at the very least travelled to Lisbon.

The diplomatic Albuquerque kept very close relations with each successive Portuguese consul in Zanzibar, partly because of his own political aspirations but mainly to oversee the welfare of the community. He was the 'principal promoter' of the Goan Institute and the charity association, the Goan Union. He funded a night school for disadvantaged Goans and paid for its initial expenses and teachers' salaries. He was not, however, immune to the petty partisanship which plagued the Goan community, and which, at times, turned litigious. In 1908, a civil suit was filed by Albuquerque on behalf of the members of the Society of St. Joseph and St. Francis against the business merchants D. B. Pereira and P. F. de Souza.

By 1914, Albuquerque was firmly established in the higher echelons of the consulate. Arrangements for official receptions were left in his capable hands and by 1915 he had assumed the office of vice-consul. From 1916, except for a short lapse, until 1933, he acted as Portuguese consul. He was awarded the Order of the Brilliant Star of Zanzibar for his services in combating plague, and the Portuguese decorated him with the *Ordem de Cristo*.

'FLAGS, BUNTING AND EVERGREENS': SHAPING ZANZIBARI SOCIETY

By the turn of the 19th century, Zanzibar's fortunes had greatly improved. People were 'living in luxury compared with their condition only a few years ago'. Water arrived by pipes from the interior delivered free to all in the town. Indian merchants were clothed in a manner 'they never thought of' and drove carriages in the evening. This newly formed consumer economy necessitated shoemakers, tailors, milliners, hosieries, draperies, crockery, cutlery, fine wines and provisions, all of which were provided for by upmarket Goan retailers.

Zanzibar developed an engaging culture of musical interludes, theatrical productions put up by amateur dramatic clubs, and the formation of numerous sports and cultural clubs. Goans played a vital part in the creation of this Eurocentric culture. At least one Goan businessman Agapitus de Souza was known to loan chairs for public events held at the Victoria Gardens. On Saturdays, between five and six in the evening, the Sultan's Goan band played at the Mnazi Moja Club. While the band performed its regular programme of waltzes and polkas at the Victoria Gardens, 'one of the most enjoyable incidents in the Zanzibar week', Pedro Francisco de Souza served liquors, teas and ices to 'thirsty members returning from the arduous pursuit of golf or tennis'.

The Goan publican had always played his part in creating affable shared public spaces. Even before the advent of clubs in Zanzibar, C. R. de Souza had converted the upper room of his establishment into a bar. British administrator Frederick Jackson often met the British consul Claude MacDonald there for a whiskey-soda. Writer F. D. Ommanney, in his recollections of Zanzibar wrote endearingly of one Goan publican who acted as host to all the patrons, watched over them carefully, 'welcomed them in and shepherded them out'.

Music, food and drink were not the only pursuits Goans took the lead in. Initially, 'the Parsis alone practiced the game of cricket', seen pitching a ball on Mnazi Moja grounds but the game did not gain prominence until Goans established a club in 1897. Shortly after, there emerged a Zanzibar Cricket Club, Parsi Cricket Club and Khoja Cricket Club. In 1919, Dr M. F. de Albuquerque donated a shield for an annual Indian intercommunity championship.

A few Goan families in Zanzibar led lives typical of the European social elite. They spoke fluent Portuguese; the inflections soft and studied. Language and religion became the civilisational boundary between Goans and other Asians. These families holidayed in Europe to recuperate from the hardship and disease of Africa. Firstborn sons studied law or medicine in London, Paris or Portugal - D. B. Pereira's son Daniel Viegas Pereira passed his bar exam in London and then proceeded to Lisbon to study Portuguese law - and their obsessive conspicuous consumption took the form of extravagant weddings and parties, priceless gifts and lavish homes.

Of those grand weddings, two that made Zanzibar come alive were that of Pedro Francisco de Souza and Emmelina Pereira, and Dr Andrade and Bertha Maria Queiroz of Lisbon, dubbed the 'grandest wedding seen in Zanzibar'.

Pedro, who had been employed by C. R. de Souza and then so bitterly severed ties, married Emmelina, in 1899, the daughter of C. R. de Souza's competitor, D. B. Pereira. The wedding celebrations went on for days. The bride wore an ivory silk dress with pearl trimmings and carried a spray of natural white flowers. Iced-champagne and ice-cream flowed freely. Among the presents laid out on the table was an exquisite gold and diamond ring; a gift from the Sultan himself.

When the thirty-five year old palace veterinarian Dr Andrade wed Bertha Maria in 1900, the Sultan, declared three glorious days of feasting and holidays for distinguished employees. The Sultan's generosity included a gold necklace as a wedding present. The Aga Khan presented a silver table service. Not to be outdone, the newly-wed Pedro Francisco de Souza forked out money for a pearl and sapphire necklace. Even Eugene Barretto, the postmaster on a government salary, splashed out on a silver belt and buckle.

In 1904, the community established the Goan Institute. Here, they reinforced their cultural and national identity with commemorations. A typical subscription ball would find the institute hall gaily decorated with flags, bunting and evergreens. After the guests were welcomed, the Portuguese anthem played and speeches delivered, the band would start playing by nine in the evening and continue till the early hours of morning. A love of theatre produced the Zanzibar Goan Dramatic Society which would perform at the Victoria Gardens.

Zanzibar's prosperity came to be reflected in its architectural landscape. There rose the spires of Christ Church and St. Joseph's Cathedral. St. Joseph's mission was first established in 1860 and within two years handed over to the Holy Ghost Fathers. In 1883 it was raised into an Apostolical Vicariate. Monsignor de Courmont was nominated by the Holy See, as Bishop of Zanzibar. From then, the church had steadily grown, owing to the increasing prosperity of the place, 'attracting to it a large number of Goanese', whose lives, although bound to Goa, had also begun to take root in Zanzibar. There were births

Main Road, Zanzibar, c.1900. 'Mention must be made of D. B. Pereira's palatial building, on the Mnazi Moja road, which is nearing completion. The house which is a two-storied building is one of the best in Zanzibar and commands a magnificent situation, having the Victoria Gardens at its front, of which it has a full view and the sea at its back. Two spacious verandahs supported by five massive Doric capital give the building a handsome appearance and the only one of its kind in Zanzibar. Mr Pereira must be congratulated on erecting such an ornamental building, thus adding to the beauty of the city'.
The Zanzibar Gazette, 21 November, 1900.

39

Victoria Gardens, Zanzibar. A culture of music, theatre and public meetings grew around Victoria Hall and Gardens. Goans were an integral part of this culture.

to be celebrated and deaths to be mourned. In September 1895, prominent Goans – C. R. de Souza, D. B. Pereira, A. M. de Albuquerque, Reginaldo de Souza, L. M. de Souza, Dr F. P. de Noronha and Felicio Dias - funded the new Catholic cemetery.

An expanding parish had necessitated a move to a larger church. By 1896, with the blueprint for a magnificent cathedral, a 'massive, dignified, cruciform structure', drawn up by the French architect Berengier of Marseilles, the Goans, as the most numerous adherents to the Roman Catholic faith, were enlisted to prepare the site for the stone-laying ceremony. And they did so, in their 'own special style with flags, bunting and ever-greens'. If there was a minor irritant during the ceremony, it was the exploding crackers they set off at odd intervals. Goan munificence was apparent in the cathedral by way of a large bell donated by C. R. de Souza. The Goan brand of Catholicism with its unwavering belief in an Abrahamic, monotheistic God brought to them by the Portuguese was intermingled with an indigenous, polytheistic need to be equally loyal to numerous village saints. And their faith articulated itself in colourful, noisy and frequent celebrations in the streets, accompanied always by the exuberant playing of the Sultan's Goan band.

A lay body, the Catholic Association of Zanzibar, emerged presided over by Dr Andrade. They groomed their own orchestra drawing on five members from the Sultan's band. The rituals of the Church merged seamlessly with their social life. Weddings, christenings and honouring long-suffering, martyred Catholic saints, all called for enthusiastic singing and dancing 'the old Goan country dances'.

Goan architectural contribution to Zanzibar was not confined to religious buildings. In other ways, too, they left their imprint. D. B. Pereira for instance, had an eye for the aesthetic - his thirty-two bed Hotel Kitaruni was a beautiful L-shaped building with enclosed manicured gardens – and in 1900, he built a palatial two-storey house on Mnazi Moja Road. Its frontal façade had five massive Doric columns rising like giants, supporting a verandah looking onto the Victoria Gardens. An open-handed benefactor of charities, Pereira played the patriarchal Godfather, throwing grand parties for his Swahili and Comoros neighbours.

In agriculture and husbandry too, Goans would leave an impact. In the early months of 1904, Dr Andrade landed six buffaloes from Goa and put them to work on his *shamba* at Sheriff Moosa and the plantation at Koani, the finest plantation on the island with trees imported from Sri Lanka, China and India. Along with the buffaloes came three Goan farmhands whose guttural instructions seemed to be perfectly comprehensible to the animals. The introduction of the hardy Indian buffalo into Zanzibar provided a fillip to agricultural production.

In Zanzibar, civic causes became a shared responsibility. Whether it was an ad hoc entertainment committee putting on a play for the War Relief Fund or the formation of a society for the prevention of cruelty against animals, representatives from various ethnic minorities played a participative role. One notable effort was in 1917, when the Indian National Association, and members of the Goan and Arab communities held a meeting at Victoria Hall to consider Dr Copeland's proposal for a Zanzibar Maternity Association. When it materialised, it was funded by Arab and Indian philanthropists.

Spared the pressure to become a settler colony, racial tensions slackened in Zanzibar, and the island assumed a 'colourful demographic character'.

42

MOMBASA
'POORLY CONCEIVED, BADLY MANAGED': THE IBEAC YEARS

'At the time when the government took over the administration from the British East Africa Company, the Goans were first on the field…having themselves obtained employment they acquainted their relatives and friends in India of the fact till almost all the vacancies were filled with their own countrymen'.

Anonymous letter in the African Standard, 21 November, 1903.

Mombasa grew with all the bluster of its native name *Kisiwa Mvita* which in Swahili means Isle of War. The harbour, 'the finest in East Africa', was about three-quarters of a mile in length, used largely by lateen-sail dhows, which arrived with the trade winds.

An old Portuguese fort guarded the channel separating Mombasa from the mainland. The mainland promised an abundance of rubber, beeswax, hides, gum, tobacco, sugarcane, wild indigo, but its most valuable export was ivory. British imperial hawks circled the skies for a long time, protective of trading rights, but remained wary of making any financial commitments in the region. When Sir William Mackinnon stepped in with his Imperial British East Africa Company, whose 'principle object' was to 'secure paramount influence,' it suited the British Crown perfectly. Indeed, the claim that had it not been for the IBEAC's 'energetic action', national interests in the region would have been 'placed in very great peril,' was not altogether an exaggeration.

In the tradition of the East India Company, the IBEAC enjoyed a royal charter and a much 'promised concession' by the Sultan of Zanzibar to administer a coastline of nearly 700 miles, which included Mombasa. In October 1888, the chief administrator of the IBEAC, George Mackenzie arrived in Mombasa, and was 'welcomed by the natives in public *durbar*'. The presumption of indigenous enthusiasm proved premature but there were other players keen on British imperial expansion into East Africa. Already, Mackenzie was assured by Asian traders in Zanzibar, of moving their businesses to Mombasa if conditions proved favourable. Souza, Junior & Dias and L. M. de Souza[1] were amongst the first to open branches.

Goan clerk with porters, Zanzibar, c.1890. Prior to the railway, human porterage facilitated trade with the interior of Africa. They carried rubber and ivory to the coast and textiles and other imports to the interior. Goan clerks were tasked with registering porters, supervising provisions and disbursing wages. Goan traders supplied Europeans with porters. Porters endured arduous conditions.

The IBEAC administration if high in spirits was low on numbers. John Ainsworth, the son of a Manchester trader, arrived to find 'there were no houses available for the staff', so they pitched tents or made other makeshift arrangement in the Ndia Kuu area of Mombasa. Ainsworth was an old hand at African affairs. He had first arrived in Africa in 1884, as a young man of twenty, employed by a trading company in the Congo. Five years later he joined the ill-fated IBEAC. His association with imperial affairs would endure and culminate with his appointment in 1918 as chief native commissioner. Ainsworth would play an important role in Goan affairs and he, in turn, was dependent on Goans.

By 1889, the IBEAC infrastructure began to take shape, but despite Mackenzie's determined plan to open up the country as speedily as possible, human porterage remained the only option which enabled trade with the interior. It became fairly obvious early on, that the inland caravan trade route could not be sustained; the cost of safaris was enormous. Each man paid in advance, carrying about 70 lbs and his provisions, cost the Company £200 per ton. The return on ivory did not always sustain the huge expense. Hence, a railway to the interior was the only solution.

The railway, politicians and capitalist pundits assured the public, 'crushes out every other system of carriage'. It was more than mere carriage; it was a moral imperative. It would destroy the slave trade and the need for human porterage. More importantly, it would encourage European imports and increase exports from the interior. But in England, the railway mustered only damp enthusiasm. The *Daily News* called it 'a wild goose chase' cautioning that, 'if it will pay, it will be made by private enterprise and if it will not, it ought not to be made at all'.

In the end, the IBEAC proved ineffectual; 'poorly conceived, badly managed and grossly undercapitalised,' the Company was destined to a short existence and in 1895 the Crown revoked its charter rights.

The IBEAC's chief redeeming virtue however, had been its recruitment of men steeped in African affairs. The British administration with characteristic vision retained these loyalists when it took over the territory as the British East Africa Protectorate. Acting Commissioner Clifford H. Craufurd explained to the Foreign Office that only 'the best men were kept' while those found wanting had been retired. The IBEAC's skeletal clerical staff had included Peregrino Caetano Antonio Lobo as clerk and Augusto Costantino Castelino as book-keeper, both having joined the Company in 1890.

Admittedly then, Lobo and Castelino had proven their merit, for they were retained by the British administration and went on to have favourable careers; Lobo as a store-keeper with the public works department and Castelino as a clerk with the treasury.

Castelino and Lobo's life however could not have been exempt from racial bias. Craufurd, who recommended the continuation of their pension insisted that Europeans suffer considerably on account

---

[1] The East Africa Stores was established in 1898 by Domingo Jeronimo dos Remedios (D. J. dos Remedios) in partnership with Luis Manuel de Souza (L. M. de Souza) but the partnership was dissolved. L. M. de Souza also traded under his own name and operated in Nairobi under East Africa Stores. In 1906, Souza consolidated all his businesses under the banner of East Africa Stores. Souza died in 1909 but the business continued. Remedios continued to trade in Mombasa as East Africa Stores. Remedios died on 16 April 1916.

East Africa Protectorate nominal roll, Mombasa, 1899. Employees of the Imperial British East Africa Company (IBEAC) taken over by the British East Africa Protectorate after the IBEAC's charter was revoked in 1895. The names of A. C. Castellino and P. C. A. Lobo can be seen on the list; both joined the IBEAC in 1890.

of the climate and as such should be paid the 'highest rate of pension', and Asians should be given a scale slightly 'inferior to that of Europeans'.

The work of a subordinate clerk in those early years was far from being an office job; it was arduous and on the move. Among its myriad of responsibilities was the recruitment of local labour, registration, supervision of rations and managing transportation. Doubtless such tasks required physical endurance, and a rudimentary knowledge of the cultural and geographical terrain. In this respect, Asian clerks had an advantage over their white colleagues. The supervising officers thought certain duties were 'those of a subordinate and not that of an officer, entailing as it does menial labour'. In such ways, Asians became essential to the machinery of empire. Yet, success was always attributed to the British officer in charge. Asians remained invisible, as officers lionised their own role in reports despatched to the Foreign Office.

A list compiled in 1899 shows the salary scales at the turn of the century. At the lower end were the district clerks at remote stations earning between Rs 125 to Rs 150 per month. The high earning Goans were employed in more prominent departments, such as the treasury, customs or attached to a sub-commissioner's office, earning between Rs 150 to Rs 300 per month. Grading and longevity of service also determined pay. It was not unusual at this time for Goans to hold supervisory posts of superintendent, head clerk or head store-keeper.

District Clerk Mervyn
Maciel hunting
at Marsabit
c.1950s.

'BEAR A MANLY HEART': GOAN FRONTIERSMEN

The notion of the cowardly Goan prevailed amongst the British, in no small part manufactured by explorer Sir Richard Burton. His lifelong dislike of the 'half-breed', the 'neither fish nor fowl nor good red herring', had led him to condemn Goans as emasculated and 'degraded'. This view agreed with an earlier House of Commons condemnation of Goans, in 1832, as a race 'least fitted for soldiers'. But in those early days of empire building in British East Africa, when both resources and men were scarce, the luxury of choosing one's soldiers did not exist; employees of the civil establishment, regardless of their profession, were expected to 'bear a manly heart in time of danger'.

In 1896, Acting Commissioner Clifford H. Craufurd proposed a volunteer corps which would equip men with cursory military training to protect the 'safety of the lives and property of the people of Mombasa'. If Craufurd is to be believed, British and British Indian subjects were willing to cooperate in 'any work of defence that might be necessary'. Sudden 'outbreaks of hostility' left Mombasa vulnerable, if the regular troops were engaged elsewhere. Of the 121 men who signed up by November 1896, only thirty-nine were European. The rest were Asian; R. Cardoza, J. C. Almeida, R. Pereira and at least seventeen other Goans were amongst those who enlisted.

The movement did not find a footing in Mombasa largely because Mombasa did not have a shooting range. It was Nairobi, where the idea found support among white settlers coming in from South Africa, encouraged by Commissioner Donald Stewart, himself a soldier, and by the enactment of the 1905 East Africa Volunteer Reserve Ordinance. The Nairobi volunteer corps was as much a part of the town's social life as was the Turf (racing) club. Every member had to be of 'European parentage over sixteen years of age' and enrolled to take an oath of allegiance. Occasionally, the muscular power of the corps would be on display; its members parading near the Town Hall with their army-style regalia of 'rifle, oil-bottle, pull-through and the full balance of ammunition issued'.

The ordinance was amended in 1907 to include 'a Goanese or Parsi'. Goans or Parsis were not allowed to join the European volunteer corps but could form a 'separate company' under the charge of a

D.B 12 bore gun popular amongst registered Goan gun-owners, advertised on *The Pioneer*, 13 June, 1908.

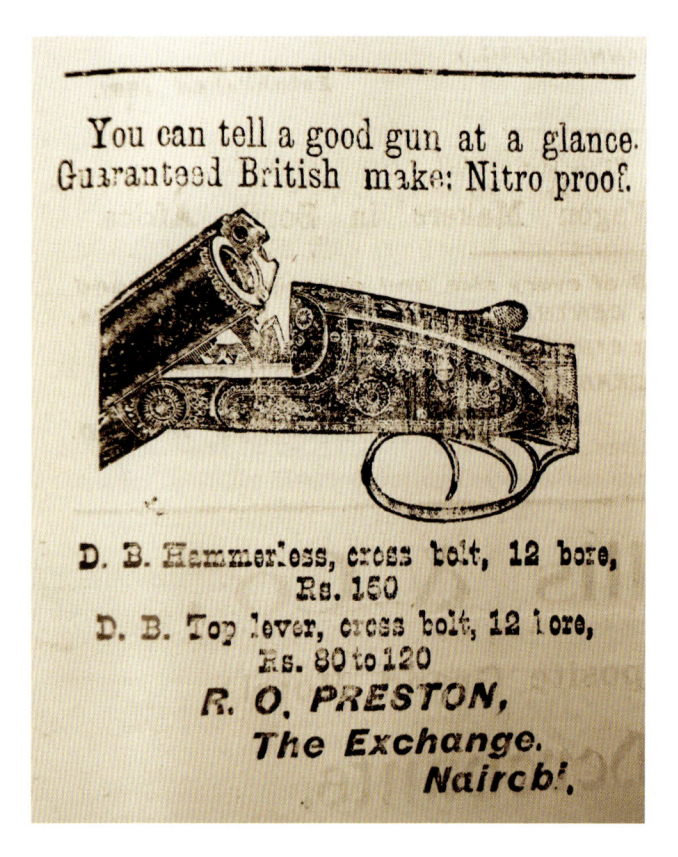

> You can tell a good gun at a glance.
> Guaranteed British make: Nitro proof.
>
> D. B. Hammerless, cross bolt, 12 bore,
> Rs. 160
> D. B. Top lever, cross bolt, 12 bore,
> Rs. 80 to 120
> R. O. PRESTON,
> The Exchange.
> Nairobi.

European officer. It is unlikely Goans showed great solidarity with the volunteer movement but Austin Rangel, a clerk with the traffic department of the Uganda Railway, did take charge of the Goan Volunteer Corps. Practice sessions were held every Friday, Saturday and Sunday afternoon at the railway range for those 'desirous to go out and shoot'. Since they risked being disbanded if their membership fell short of fifteen, presumably the minimum requirement had been met.

There was a real sense of the East Africa protectorate being frontier land and Goans were part of the rough-hewn culture that went with it. As registered gun owners, they owned a long double-barrelled 12 bore shotgun and were not averse to carrying a pistol. Quite apart from individuals owning guns, mostly for hunting, companies too registered firearms. In Mombasa, the firm of Souza Junior & Dias owned two DB shotguns, and businessman D. L. Pereira[2] owned an array of firearms; one DB shotgun, one Webley revolver and one Winchester rifle. Having businesses in more than one location prompted multiple gun ownership. Braganza & Viegas in Mumias were registered owners of six Snider rifles for 'caravan use'. They may have been caravan agents or caravan leaders, using the guns to protect porters while transporting goods on foot.

---

[2] Diogo Luis Pereira was a well respected Mombasa merchant who initially partnered with Augusto Francisco Pereira under the trade name of A & D Pereira. The partnership was dissolved in 1897, but A & D continued as a business entity. D. L. Pereira traded under his own name.

'ALL CLASSES ASSEMBLED': CREATING A PUBLIC CULTURE

As far as the British empire went, Mombasa was not a cosmopolitan city on the scale of Calcutta but it was not without its own cultural and ethnic diversity. By 1896, it could boast of 107 Europeans among which were English, Germans, Greeks and Romanians, 169 Goans and Eurasians, 5,962 Indians, 596 Arabs and 14,574 Swahilis. Three years later, the Goan population had ballooned considerably enough for Dr Luis Lobo to have been appointed president of the Goan Community. In 1905, Portugal appointed him consular agent; he had formerly served as a district health officer in Goa.

Despite their lack of any real political agency, Goans were instrumental in creating a public culture of biracial cohesion and collaboration. The earliest manifestation of a shared public space was M. R. de Souza's store established in 1889, at a time when IBEAC staff looked for social interaction in a lonely port town. The staff met regularly at Souza's store for groceries, beers (Souza was the sole agent for Allsopp's and Tuborg beer) or mineral water. John Ainsworth in his memoirs remembered it referred to as 'The Club' and a place where one could 'always get a cold lunch'. These regular high-spirited gatherings became the nucleus of the Mombasa Club.

Meanwhile, Goans had been meeting at a Customs House *godown*, and in 1901 formed their own Goan Reading Room. Likely, the preponderance of Goans employed by customs as clerks and in supervisory positions, facilitated the letting of Customs House *godowns* to be used as meeting places. The superintendent of customs at Leven House Mombasa was John Baptiste Faria, who had joined the colonial establishment in 1895. In a more senior post, as head *godown* keeper, was Manuel Salvador D'Souza, who had joined in 1899. But also, the chief of customs was an honorary member of the Reading Room, and likely the British establishment had encouraged its founding.

Eventually, for their gatherings, they were generously allowed the use of the top floor in a building owned by D. L. Pereira on Ndia Kuu, at a monthly rent of Rs 20. It was during this period, as the name of the association implied, a culture of reading spread. Colonial papers and books in various languages were donated and made available to members. Within a decade, the association came to 'possess a very

Main Road, Mombasa, c.1907. On the right can be seen the Mombasa studio of Coutinho and Sons photographers. The Handbook for East Africa, 1905, lists the following pioneer Goan businesses in Mombasa: Souza Junior & Dias; East Africa Stores; M. R. de Souza Stores; the tailor D. D. Souza; E. N. J. D'Souza; the photographer D. V. Figueira; T. Siqueira Merchant; Edward St. Rose Chemists.

Right
M. R. de Souza stores advertised in *The Pioneer*, 25 April, 1908.

Far right
M. R. de Souza gravestone, Nairobi South Cemetery. Souza died in 1906. The business was then managed by his wife and family.

M. R. de SOUZA,
ESTABLISHED 1889.
TAILOR AND OUTFITTER.
BOOT AND SHOE MAKER.
DRAPER AND HOSIER.
Caps, Hats, Shirts &c. &c. in great Variety.
IMPORTER OF WINES, SPIRITS, OIL MAN'S STORES, &c. OF THE BEST QUALITY.
SAFARI OUTFITS A SPECIALITY.
London Offices:—
119 to 125 Finsbury Pavement, E. C
Branches:—NAIROBI, NAKURU and MOMBASA

valuable library'. Women, though few, enjoyed a fair degree of independence and could join the men at community events. They appeared always 'finely dressed, some in European style'. By 1911, a 'Bachelors' Cottage' provided entertainment with Mrs Rozario and Mrs D'Mello singing *mandos* in soprano. One contemporary commentator, J. C. D'Mello remarked that 'the presence of ladies was the essential part of a society'. This nod to gender equality further likened Goans to their European counterparts.

However, the bulk of Goans fell outside the ambit of this exclusivist elite culture. Membership of the Goan Reading Room remained small (sixty-four members by 1903) and restricted by status, occupation or caste. For those Goans, who were members, the minutiae of daily existence took priority over any deeper engagement in political or philosophical polemics. Decades later, the editor of the (East Africa) *Goan Voice* was to lament that 'the individual [Goan] ambition is of amassing a small fortune, building a house, retiring from active service and sitting pretty'.

The *godown* continued to be used for the plays the Reading Room performed. These were looked forward to by the entertainment-deprived Goans and Europeans alike. Their audiences included leading merchants and officials of the protectorate. In December 1904, Sub-Commissioner John Ainsworth and his wife, along with Sub-Commissioner Lane and the German Vice-Consul Dr Brode, had occupied the reserved seats at a rather uninspiring performance of *'The castle of Andalusia'*. Included in the cast were 'many new actors: Rosario, Fernandes, Salter, Mascarenhas, Makertich'. The previous year had seen an even grander 'operatic performance' by the Goan Reading Room, where amongst the European audience were the merchant family Boustead, protectorate Auditor W. A. Bowring, and Superintendent of Police Raymond M. Ewart. The opening chorus of *'Awake oh happy nation,'* sung as an amicable quartet exemplified the collaborative nature of the evening. The chief engineer of the steam ship *Juba*, Francis Byrnes gave a spirited solo on the banjo. Other cast members included a Mr Thoy, Durante D'Souza, Anselmo D'Sa, John Lopes and Castello Branco. The performances mounted were mostly farces and lacked finesse but more admirable than theatrical ability was the biracial make-up of the cast; Europeans and Goans together on stage. The audiences, at times, tended to get carried away, fuelled by drink, and rowdy interruptions were common.

This racial crossover which the Goans fostered and sustained partly because the British erroneously thought of them as Portuguese 'half-castes', did not extend to indigenous populations; rarely, if ever, did Goans socialise with Africans. But Goans were not averse to cross-cultural cohabitation and sexual liaisons with indigenous populations, particularly in the interior, away from the censorious glare of the township community.

In 1903, D. L. Pereira who had so generously fostered the Goan Reading Room, offered his premises for hosting the founding committee meeting of the Mombasa Public Library. Present during the meeting were Judge Ralph P. B. Cator, who led the project and High Court Pleader, Cavasji Dalal, who informed that Rs 2,000 had been pledged as donations. On 11 January, 1904, about a hundred people of 'all classes assembled' near Dalal's office, and being led by Cator walked to Adamji Allibhai's house, where vice-president of the library Dewji Jamal and committee member Dr L. A. Gama Rose, a young, energetic, newly-arrived Goan physician, received them. Cator then declared the library officially opened. Its collection of books, perhaps modest, contained papers and magazines from India, Goa, Lisbon, England, South Africa and Zanzibar. Once the public library became accessible, it was at times, used as a venue for Goan Reading Room meetings.

In 1911, dismissed members of the Goan Reading Room proposed setting up a 'Goan Institute' amidst protests and fears that such a move would 'damage the status of the community and only serve to satisfy the selfish ends of a few dissatisfied individuals'. Protest notwithstanding, the Goan Reading Room did, in 1914, become the Goan Institute, Mombasa.

The Mombasa Goan community with men of letters amongst them, by 1903, had started the monthly journal *O Anglo-Goano* at a subscription rate of Rs 4 per annum. Hardly a trace of it survives and its existence might have been brief, but other legacies of their print work remain. They were employed in good numbers in colonial newspaper establishments mostly as compositors. *The East African Standard*, for instance, had in 1907 as 'foreman of the works', one Lobo, who proposed 'an enthusiastically received' toast to the prosperity of the *Standard* during a shindig at the editor's house. Of the thirty staff present on that evening, quite a few must have been Goan for songs were sung in 'English, Portuguese, Goanese, Hindustani and native tongues'.

A relationship of mutual respect resulted in the editor of the *East Africa and Uganda Mail* being made an honorary member of the Goan Reading Room. Nonetheless, Goans at times infuriated newspaper editors with their letters of complaints and on one occasion at least, the *Standard* demanded they mend their ways or risk being boycotted. Acid retaliatory letters and counter-threats were always swift from the community as they were in this instance. The *Standard* was told in no uncertain terms that their threats were 'quite immaterial and of very little importance'. At the time, no editor, and particularly not that of the *Standard*, could seriously think of boycotting Goans, dependent as the papers were on the advertising revenue from retailers such as M. R. de Souza and Souza Junior & Dias. Equally important, were the distribution networks Goan retailers provided to newspapers.

It was not just privately owned newspapers that relied on Goans; the government did as well. The head compositor in 1902 at the government printing press was Francis Xavier Fernandes and his assistant was Antonio Caetano Monteiro. Compositor John Marcel Dias and pressman Hylario Antonio Cunha were also part of the team. Fernandes was the first to join in May 1898, followed by Monteiro in September of the same year.

Another public space Goans supported financially was the Holy Ghost Chapel. The Monsignor de Courmont accompanied by the energetic Father Alexander le Roy, both of the Holy Ghost Fathers had, in 1889, established the Catholic mission of St. Joseph at Ndera. That same year, Roy had conducted the first Catholic baptism in Mombasa; Diego and Natalie Pereira's daughter Maria. Roy spent the next two years exploring the coast for possible locations to establish missions but returned to Mombasa in 1891, and sought the hospitality of Pereira again, from whom he bought a house. With the house renovated and serving as a chapel, the Catholic mission marked its commencement but the Holy Ghost Fathers despaired at the numbers evangelised. Roy's successor Father Flick noted: 'apart from the Goans, the only Catholics in Mombasa are those at the mission'. The year 1897 proved more favourable when a plot of five acres was finally purchased at £30 an acre, for a new chapel.

Goans continued to be pillars of the Catholic church; among those early church worthies was I. J. J. Maciel[2] as parish choir master and Saturnino de Souza as general organiser. The Catholic Church and the Goan Reading Room had overlapping social lives; the Holy Ghost Fathers were frequent guests at community events.

Mostly Goan contributions to the church remained invisible or attributed solely to the efforts of white missionaries. When in 1899, the famine-struck Wanyika began to arrive in Mombasa, Father Ball of the Catholic mission furnished them with 'thirty pounds of rice and thirty pounds of seed corn'. Acting

---

[2] I.J.J. Maciel joined the treasury department of the civil establishment in 1897. Saturnino de Souza was the chief clerk with the C.M.S.

The christening of Edward Pereira at the Holy Ghost Chapel, 1915. Left Dominic Caetano Pereira with wife Basilia Carmelina Pereira, and Augustino Pereira. Basilia is seen holding her new born son who in later life became a Kenyan nationalist.

Commissioner Craufurd, overwhelmed by this 'philanthropic conduct', made mention of it in a letter to the Foreign Office. What he failed to mention was that at the heart of mission charity lay Goan generosity by way of donations eked from their meagre salaries. Nonetheless, on one occasion when these monthly subscriptions proved too onerous, the Goans threatened to bring their own priest from Goa to tend to their pastoral needs.

In 1912, the departing Bishop Allgeyer, whose evangelising zeal was responsible for much of the spread of Roman Catholicism in British East Africa, and who had presided over countless Goan weddings, funerals and celebrations beginning in Zanzibar, was presented by the Mombasa parishioners, largely Goan, with a carved sandalwood teapoy, a tablecloth embroidered in gold, two flower vases, an ivory paper knife, a silver pen holder, a silver ink stand and a silver-framed photo.

Mathias J. Maciel and Josephine D'Sa, 1926, married at the Holy Ghost Cathedral, Mombasa. The cathedral was consecrated in 1923. Wedding receptions usually took place at a friend's house or at a Goan store.

'IRREPROACHABLE CHARACTER': THE WORKING POOR

The usual chatter at the European Mombasa Club might have fallen silent on 16 March, 1904, for the familiar figure of chief steward, J. D. Lobo was no more.

Lobo had first left the shores of Goa in 1880, as a steward working on board the Royal Navy. Twelve years later, he became known to the residents of Mombasa as E. J. Berkeley's head butler. Berkeley at the time served as the administrator of the Imperial British East Africa Company and after his appointment as commissioner for Uganda, Lobo once again returned to the navy where he served as wardroom steward on board the *H. M. S. Blanche*. In 1896, he joined the Mombasa Club as chief steward; a much-loved personality of 'irreproachable character and manners', fondly known as 'Old Lobo'. Upon his death, the members of the club took out a subscription for his widow in Goa.

Hardly any trace remains of the historical lives of the working poor – the Goan stewards, tailors, *dhobis*, shoemakers and cooks who worked in East Africa. Not given to keeping records or writing journals, their narrative has withered away. If their stories appear at all, they are relegated a cameo role as menials to administrators, missionaries or explorers, or worse, as delinquent offenders in court records. Nonetheless, these instances do provide us a glimpse into their lives. For instance, the case of *dhobi* (laundryman) Khaitan Fernandes in 1903 shows how very little agency the working class had, and how much they depended on the goodwill of those in positions of power. Khaitan, it was alleged, had failed to return a shirt belonging to Captain C. Laughlin of the 4th battalion, King's African Rifles, or rather that the shirt which had been returned was of an inferior quality.

Laughlin took Khaitan to court, where Khaitan was ordered to pay Rs 5 for the shirt and an additional Rs 4 for court costs. While these costs would have been a financial strain on Khaitan, they had little impact on Laughlin who donated the money to the 'poor box'. The object of the exercise had been only to render a 'lesson for the *dhobi*'.

The instance of J. Lobo, also in 1903, employed as a domestic servant by the Italian merchant G. Gheradi Angiolini, relates the sort of life a working class man might have led. Lobo was put in charge of Angiolini's *shamba* at Kilindini, overseeing the livestock of buffaloes and fowls. In a complicated case, Angiolini accused Lobo of stealing livestock. Lobo was sentenced to one month in jail and fined Rs 150. Lobo would hardly have been in a position to defend himself given his lack of proficiency in English and yet he either chose to, or was compelled to, act as his own lawyer. The only defence witness Lobo could provide was the Mauritian woman he was living with at the time.

Elite Goans socially alienated the working poor excluding them from their clubs. But there was a growing sense that their welfare was a collective responsibility. In August 1908, the community came together to form the Goan Union. With leading Mombasa Goan merchants 'supporting the movement', this charitable organisation sought to mitigate the misfortunes of the poor.

'CARRY ON THE BUSINESS': WOMEN PIONEERS

Women are relegated to the periphery of the Goan migration narrative. Like most migrations, it was young men who ventured forth and returned home to seek a wife once they had made their way, if not their fortune. Once married, they returned to Africa, alone, leaving behind newly-wed brides. Their numbers might have been few, but those women bold enough to accompany men to Africa did play a significant role in nurturing the community.

The declining fortunes of Portugal and the stagnant Goan economy, made an East African Goan groom a prized catch even amongst the landed gentry. So keen was the demand that girls were often affianced to men they had never met. If they were lucky they might have seen a faded photograph or encountered a close relative on whose character reference the alliance would be secured.

Yet these arrangements were not loveless marriages. They were sustained by a deep Catholic faith in the benevolence of God. A sense of duty and family honour called for lifelong monogamy and ensured every effort was made to make the relationship work. And then, there were children to bind even the most incompatible marriage. Beyond honour and obligation, these were men and women, mostly sexually inexperienced, who delighted in each other in an otherwise isolating world. The women, particularly, felt a genuine joy in being liberated from hemmed-in Goan villages. Here, they endured deprivations but thrived.

As with most early twentieth century marital relations, Goan wives were subordinated to their husbands. The marriage, in many ways, was a transfer of custodial responsibility from father to husband. The girls would at best have had a few years of learning at a chapel school which would hardly have prepared them for an emancipated life. Women were expected to rear children, teach them catechism and tend to household chores with the assistance of a 'houseboy' or cook. For the most part their lack of language proficiency in English or Swahili confined them to the house, but they did accompany their husbands to remote districts into the interior and showed great capacity for independent thought and action, as in the case of Ezalda Clara Albuquerque.

Ezalda Clara Albuquerque with husband Caetano Jose Dias and children, c.1910.

C. J. Dias and children, c.1920.

C. J. Dias, second right standing, with friends, c.1920. Women although few in numbers were integral to nurturing the Goan pioneer community in East Africa.

Ezalda and her husband Caetano Jose Dias, fifteen years her senior, operated a timber mill in Eldama Ravine, some 400 miles into the interior from Mombasa. She came from a prominent Candolim family; one of her sisters was a doctor. In Eldama, Ezalda learnt to drive a tractor and ride a horse. She helped out with the wood logging and being a crack-shot, enjoyed hunting small game with her double-barrel shotgun. She was also a booklover, a passion she shared with her second husband Peter Zuzarte who had previously fathered a child – Joseph Murumbi who later became independent Kenya's second vice-president – with a Masai woman. Ezalda married Peter after Dias died in 1928.

The custom of young girls being married off to financially stable but much older husbands, meant that often, they outlived their partners. There are several instances of women in East Africa who upon their husband's death were declared administratrices of their estates. This was no doubt purely a legal matter; the estate was managed by an appointed lawyer or male relative. But some women did assume responsibility for the estates they inherited. Widowhood, in a very real sense, brought them financial independence.

An early example of female entrepreneurship comes from Maria Blandina Saldanha de Souza. Upon her husband Michael Rosario de Souza's death in March 1906, undaunted, she declared her intent to 'carry on the business'.

Souza died aged just forty-four and was deeply mourned by the residents of Mombasa. For years, he had been the favourite of the upper crust colonials, who had from 'the very earliest days looked to the wants of the first European residents in this country'. He had a reference letter from Commissioner Sir Charles Eliot to prove his credentials. Souza had done exceedingly well for himself. By 1900, he had a house on Hardinge Street neighbouring land owned by the wealthy merchant Dewji Jamal. Employing about thirty-five staff, the retail business expanded into Nairobi and Nakuru, and in later years, Souza spent much of his time in Nairobi, his final resting place.

Souza had died intestate; Maria, by virtue of the Portuguese civil code, inherited his estate. The business had previously survived Souza's absence. He had spent most of 1903 in Goa. Maria's involvement in the business may have been that of a figurehead while male relatives oversaw operations. Nonetheless, she continued as matriarch of the business, lending her name to financial dealings and court proceedings. When she retired in the mid-1920s, she executed three powers of attorney favouring Victor Saldanha, Justiniano Pereira and a joint third between Mario Pinto and her son Thomas Sebastiao Emar de Souza. This arrangement lasted until Emar consolidated his hold over the family business in the 1930s. Maria may not have enjoyed full autonomy but another equally resilient woman, Cecilia Augusta Martins, did.

Cecilia had married Albino Daniel Dias after the death of his first wife. Albino was the owner of Edward St. Rose & Co, perhaps the best known chemist in Mombasa at the time, selling patented medicines 'always fresh and of the best makers'. He had started his career in Zanzibar in 1895 as a dispenser assisting an English doctor. In 1897, he moved to Mombasa and with E. N. de Souza as partner founded Edward St. Rose & Co on Kilindini Road, by combining the names of their two respective sons. Two years later, Souza withdrew from the venture continuing his own business and Albino moved the pharmacy to Mombasa's main street of Ndia Kuu. By then, it was established enough for the proprietor to be known as 'St. Rose' although this was never his surname. It was however conveniently European sounding, a little trick more than one Goan business adopted. The Mombasa branch was under the 'personal control' of 'St. Rose' whilst the later established Nairobi branch was conducted by L. M. Coelho, a 'practical chemist from Bombay'.[1]

When Cecilia's husband died on 19 January, 1917, she inherited the business. By the following year, the death of another family member, Melinda Dias, compelled her to assume responsibility for Melinda's estate as well. Widowed at thirty-six, Cecilia eventually became a competent businesswoman owning property on Kilindini and Ganjoni Roads. She scaled down the pharmacy business but kept it afloat until her sons could take over.

---

[1] The death of a L. M. Coelho is recorded in Nairobi on 23 June, 1906. Mr D'Mello then headed the Nairobi branch of the St. Rose pharmacy.

62

NAIROBI
'SUPPLIES PORTERS': PAVING THE WAY FOR THE RAILWAY

'The proper settlement of Goans in this colony dates back to the early days of the construction of the Uganda Railway. The locomotive carried trade with it as it penetrated the interior, and the steady commercial expansion of the country served as an inducement for the Goan to settle here'.

Goan Institute Nairobi letter in The Leader of East Africa, 16 January, 1909.

Having revoked the IBEAC's charter rights in 1895, the British Crown assumed control over what became known as the British East Africa Protectorate (roughly the terrain covering present-day Kenya). The task of building a railway commenced in earnest. Of those railway towns which would emerge in Africa, Nairobi would take its place on the world stage. But before establishing Nairobi, the trail inward necessitated setting up stations - garrisons and supply depots - into the interior.

John Ainsworth was dispatched up-country to Machakos in 1892, by the Company, to soften the indigenous populations, mainly the Kamba, to imperial interests. Not renowned for his social skills, Ainsworth was nonetheless an immensely capable administrator. He sent detailed intelligence reports from Machakos. This flurry of correspondence emanating from his desk would have necessitated a clerk. To this end, he was joined by Lewis Sequeira.

The cricket-loving Sequeira from Tivim in Goa, had attended school in Pune and at twenty-one years of age set sail by dhow to Mombasa. Upon his arrival in February 1896, he was recruited to work for Sir Arthur Hardinge, the commissioner's office. Working in Hardinge's office during those early days could only have meant constant upheaval, and Sequeira was transferred to Machakos. He made the trek from Mombasa to Machakos on foot, walking over 300 miles, twelve miles a day for nearly thirty days. For company he had six *askaris*, fifty Swahili porters and two servants. When Ainsworth became sub-commissioner of Ukamba province in 1895, and subsequently took up office in Nairobi, Sequeira became his chief clerk; one of the most influential posts to hold at the time, as evidenced by his substantial annual

Uganda Railway station at Kibwezi, c.1900-1907. Asian traders flourished at Kibwezi and Mackakos before the founding of Nairobi. In 1908, Manoel de Souza of the Nairobi Bakery, requested the Uganda Railway to allow him to cultivate the garden opposite this Kibwezi railway station.

Subordinates' Quarters, Nairobi c.1901. A 1901 report described the quarters as 'all built of corrugated iron and wood' raised 3 feet from the ground on pillars of iron or stone.

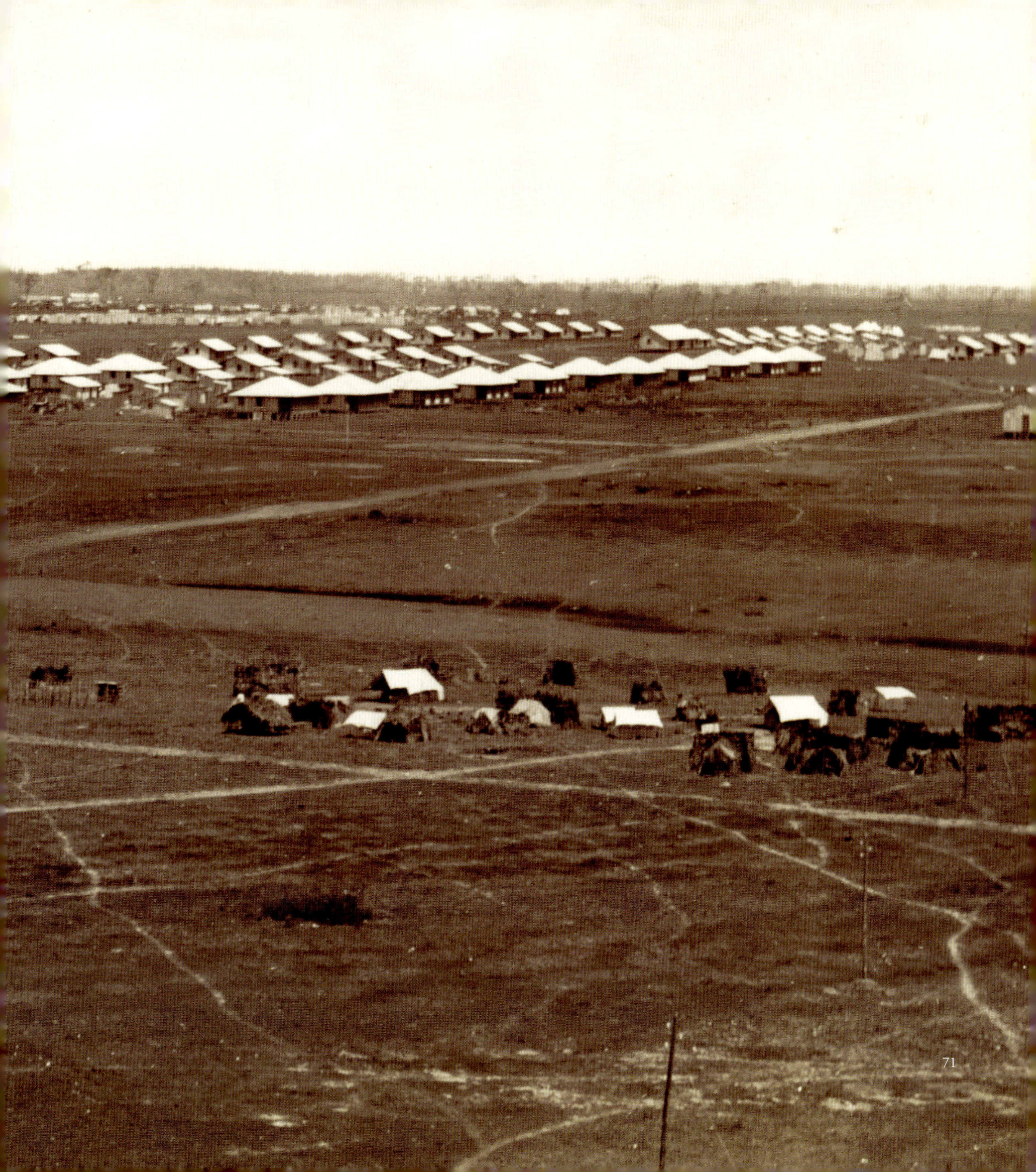

Medical staff, Nairobi, c.1901. The Uganda Railway medical staff merged with the government medical department in 1901. Goan compounders listed with the Government medical department include: Sebastiao Francisco d'Costa (1901), Felicio Luis Coelho (1902), A. Caetano Fernandes (1903), Alex H. Coelho (1903), Pedro Joao Fernandes (1904) and Alfred d'Mello (1905).

When the government granted Ribeiro land, he built a dak bungalow and carried on with his practice. He compounded an effective tablet which he patented as anti-malaria pills and sold through his own pharmacy R. Ayres & Co on Victoria Street, 'filling local and outstation prescriptions'.

Ribeiro's role expanded to include civic responsibilities as the town grew. He was regularly nominated by the sub-commissioner to be a member of the Nairobi Township Committee, instituted in 1900 to comprise of 'four of the leading merchants or other residents in the township'. In 1903 it had Edward Noronha as a member, possibly the same E. Noronha who a year later sold his debt-ridden business to Rayne and Grayman. The remit of the township committee among other things included 'policing, lighting and cleaning'. From 1905, Ribeiro was a non-official member at least until 1912, loyally attending meetings.

The uneven racial representation on the township committee (ten Europeans and two Asians by 1905) gave rise to politicking by its European members, and much of its agenda was skewed to positively impact European residents and traders. However, with whatever little influence they could exert, Ribeiro along with P. K. Ghandy, an other Asian non-official member, did put forward proposals impacting Nairobi. In August 1906, for instance, Ghandy proposed and Ribeiro seconded, 'that another hotel license should

Nairobi Indian Bazaar c.1904-1910. There were Goan shops operating in the Indian bazaar.

be granted in Nairobi'; the motion carried by six votes to one.

In the summer of 1908, Ribeiro returned from an eight month holiday in Goa, with his young bride Margarida Lourenco, the youngest daughter of a prominent lawyer. Eventually, he settled into a life of domestic bliss. His large two-storeyed house with its wooden verandah became the venue for lavish balls. On the ground floor lived an in-house tailor, to stitch clothes for Ribeiro's rapidly expanding family. And there were the many nannies each tending to a different child. The soft-spoken, stoic doctor set off every morning after breakfast and a stroll through his garden, elegantly dressed with a diamond stick-pin and a gold watch-chain, to arrive at his surgery by 9 a.m. Rosendo, who had arrived in Africa as a young man somewhat unsure of his future, would become central to life in Nairobi: as a doctor, a member of the township committee and the (Liquor) Licensing Court, as Portuguese vice-consul from 1914 – 1922, and an open-handed benefactor of the Goan community.

Indians were scapegoated for the recurrent outbreak of disease in the township. In 1902, medical officer Dr H. E. Mann had insisted that 'every effort should be made to keep the Indians (railway coolies, shopkeepers) entirely apart from the Europeans'. In his experience, Indians had proved to be so dirty that it was impossible to keep 'them and their surroundings in a sanitary condition'. Much of the alarm raised over matters of hygiene carried an element of opportunism. It served the dual purpose of marginalising Asians while encouraging Europeans to fill the gap.

When Superintendent of Public Works Baty visited the chief bakery (likely to have been Goan-owned) in the bazaar, he found the room 'in which the oven stood to be very dirty and apparently used by the baker and his family as a living and sleeping room'. Baty's proposal to erect regulated bakehouses and slaughterhouses was no doubt in the interests of the public, but invariably anxieties over hygiene led to calls for racial segregation. When the Nairobi Butchery opened in 1905, for instance, proprietor J. Janatos announced its premises would be 'rented out to Europeans in preference'.

The relocation of the Indian bazaar to the outskirts of town allowed for the flourishing of European businesses in a central location near the railway station. Along the two main thoroughfares – Victoria Street and Government Road – emerged a sprinkling of European establishments. But Goan businesses also prospered in this 'European bazaar', catering almost exclusively to a European clientele. Of those early success stories was M. R. de Souza who opened a branch in 1904 in the 'European market', Souza Junior & Dias and F. M. de Souza on Victoria Street, and L. M. de Souza on Government Road.

By 1906, the unimpeded success of Indian and Goan traders became the envy of Nairobi; fear-mongers levied the charge of the 'Asiatic trading evil', accusing them of repatriating productive capital back to India instead of reinvesting in Africa. They called openly 'for purely wholesale firms to be of European origin'.

Indian businesses did remit the bulk of their profits home but the charge was not entirely justified. A. M. Jeevanjee had built much of early Nairobi's hard infrastructure, including the sub-commissioner's house. Asians such as Alim Shah, Hira, Abdullah owned large tracts of land on either side of the river. Nearly six acres were owned by A. B. Chunha, almost certainly a corruption of the surname Cunha. The Goans, despite being a numerically insignificant community, just 591 according to the 1909 Nairobi census returns, were responsible for the construction of some splendid buildings. One of them was L. M. de Souza's new store constructed in 1906, at the time of consolidating his various enterprises under the single name of East Africa Stores. Also in 1906 Souza Junior & Dias plunged their profits into constructing the 'solidly built' Grand hotel (run by H. H. Diamond) and a store of their own. It is unlikely that Goans frequented these affluent stores but as public spaces the buildings played an important role in hosting community meetings and occasionally a Goan wedding.

Another star in its ascendancy was that of the Nazareth brothers as caterers to the Uganda Railway and operating a factory manufacturing 'A1 class aerated waters'. They would rise to spectacular prominence, when in March, 1908, their so 'fine a building' on Government Road was completed and the new store opened for business. Inside the store was a cornucopia of luxury items: a well-stocked haberdashery, *sola topees*, boots, shoes, delicacies of all kinds, fresh tobacco, soft blankets, fine fabrics, jewellery, crockery, glassware and the latest novels. Women were spared brusque male salesmen - the ladies department was under the management of a European lady. A 'good assortment of English papers and magazines was received on every mail'. The old store was converted into a restaurant; four rooms fronting the road were set aside as dining rooms reserved for Europeans, with an adjoining billiard room.

The Nazareths were of good Moira stock, a village in north Goa; sons of Caetano Vicente de Nazaré and Victoria Sebastiana. According to family sources, the neatly bearded Raphael Agostinho had arrived in 1895 and joined the Uganda Railway as a clerk. Raphael took an enterprising gamble and started a bakery. His brother Joaquim Antonio Nazareth, a burly man keen on making his fortune, soon joined him. The brothers took daring risks at a time when capital infusions and faith in the fumbling protectorate were both in scarce supply.

Joaquim Antonio Nazareth, c.1905-1915.

Opening of new Nazareth store, *The Pioneer*, 11 July, 1908.

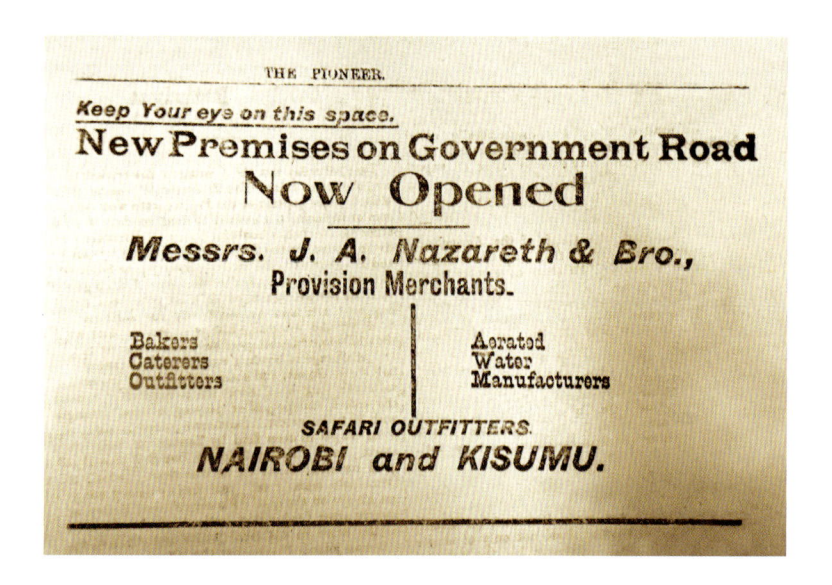

> THE PIONEER.
>
> Keep Your eye on this space.
> ## New Premises on Government Road
> ## Now Opened
>
> Messrs. **J. A. Nazareth & Bro.,**
> Provision Merchants.
>
> Bakers / Caterers / Outfitters   Aerated Water Manufacturers
>
> SAFARI OUTFITTERS.
> **NAIROBI and KISUMU.**

In 1903, A. E. Cruickshank, manager Traffic of the Uganda Railway, called for tenders for catering of the railway refreshment rooms at Nairobi and Mohoroni, and the *dak* bungalows - built a little away from the railway platforms for passengers to take their refreshments - at Voi, Makindu, Nakuru and Port Florence. The Nazareths landed a six-year Uganda Railway catering contract. With this, their fortunes soared although reviews of the food served were not always complimentary.

The Nazareths came to epitomise the very spirit of Nairobi – young, dynamic and ready to embrace challenge. Despite minor obstacles such as being charged once with supplying alcohol to a native, the brothers were well respected, and stated often, 'N stands for Nairobi, N stands for Nazareth'.[1] Their contribution went well beyond trading; they impacted the town aspect, funding civic improvements such as lighting installations. Joaquim was nominated to serve on the township committee for the year 1908.

The racially motivated calls for restrictions on non-white immigration, the curtailment of land rights, the attempts to curb Asian trade, the demands to cull Goan jobs in the British administration were all engineered to give Europeans an upper hand. Despite the uneven concentration of power, what is remarkable at this time in colonial history is the inversion of subordinate roles. It was not unusual to find Europeans in the employ of Goans. The Nazareth brothers had a private European nurse and a European store section manager; J. M. Campos hired a European woman to run his vinegar manufacturing unit; the Goan Institute proposed retaining the full-time services of a European nurse and planned to build a school putting it under the direction of a European teacher (an idea which did not bear fruition until 1930). In other ways too, Goans engaged with white society. The Nazareth brothers were on hand supervising the catering at dinners hosted by the Uganda Railway, and during the 1906 visit of the Duke and Duchess

---

[1] According to family sources, the Nazareth brothers also owned the Nairobi Silk Emporium on Government Road, Garden Bar at the end of Jevanjee Gardens, and the Metropole Hotel at the junction of River Road and the Racecourse Road.

Extract of Nairobi map, 1920, MPGG1/95, National Archives, Kew. Map shows the racial segregation of Nairobi by 1920. Area marked no. 1 was the European commercial area. Areas 2 & 3 were the Asian commerical and residential areas. J. M. Campos as municipal councillor protested at the confinement of Asians in this small area.

of Connaught; the King's African Rifles (KAR) band led by its Goan bandmaster Felicio Caetano Pinto, frequently delighted guests at these functions.

But no matter how prosperous Goans grew or how entwined their lives were with those of their white counterparts, Goan names never appeared as invitees to society receptions nor were they allowed in white-only establishments or as members of European clubs. In early 1911, several 'well-dressed Goans' arrived at the station to receive Governor Sir Percy Girouard, only to be turned away by the authorities. While Europeans were allowed unfettered access, restrictions had been placed on the number of attending Indians, and in this instance Goans were to be treated no differently.

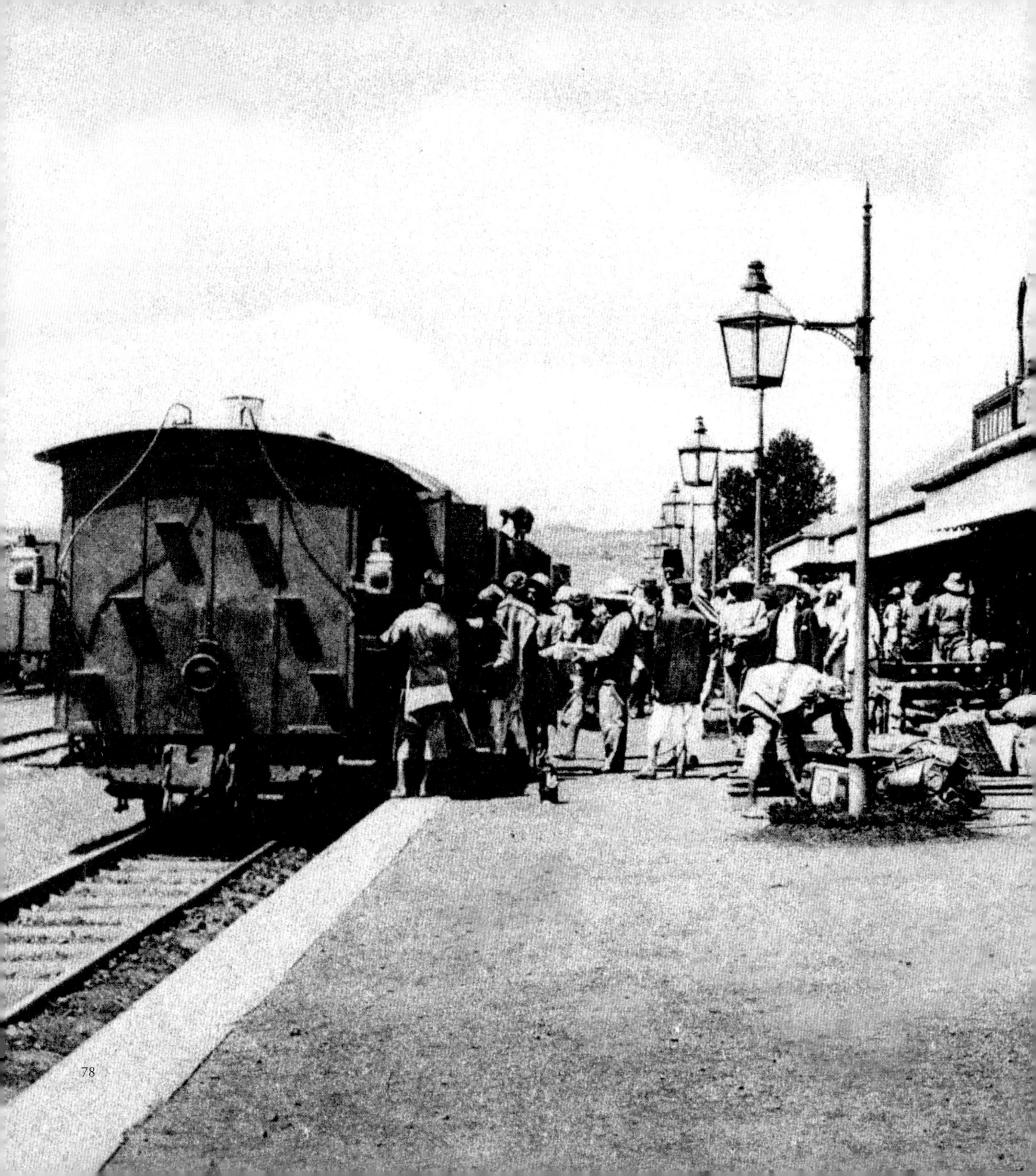

'WELL CONTESTED GAME': THE PORTUGUESE CRICKET CLUB

Most of the Goans recruited by the railway had been hired locally in Mombasa between 1896 and 1897 on temporary contracts, and paid a modest salary of fifty to eighty rupees per month. It is likely the Goans had heard about the railway construction and travelled to Mombasa anticipating employment. The reputation of Goans as reliable, trustworthy and diligent was built on the foundation laid by this initial recruitment, for although no one had drawn a plan to specifically recruit Goans, within a period of five years, the civil establishment showed a marked preference for Goan clerks.

On 28 May, 1899, the railhead reached Nairobi and on 18 July, 1899, the railway staff moved up there. The railway soon became the central pulse of Nairobi, a self-contained organism, responsible not just for transportation but for the moral, religious and social life of its staff. To the Goans, the railway provided their accommodation, it loaned one of its offices as a makeshift chapel for church services, and it provided grounds nearby for sports and recreation.

Perhaps the railway's most contentious role was that of adjudicator; a railway magistrate was appointed to deal with offences committed by its employees. Sub-Commissioner Ainsworth resented this usurpation of his own authority. By October 1899 relations between the protectorate and railway officials had soured to such an extent that they grouped on either side of the Nairobi River. There's no evidence that this rivalry between the two offices extended to Goans, even though in Nairobi, railway Goans vastly outnumbered those employed by protectorate offices. On the contrary, Goans banded together to form the Portuguese Cricket Club.

The British believed sports taught men union, discipline and self-reliance. Cricket was the premier game amongst the railway colleagues; football came a close second. As in everything else, the sports grounds were segregated. The European playing field was adjoining the railway station and nearby were the grounds made available to Goans. Its members formed the nucleus of the Portuguese Cricket Club, named accordingly to distinguish them from Indians. A 'well contested game' between the various clubs, namely the (European) Nairobi Sports Club, the Uganda Railway Indian Cricket Club and the Portuguese Cricket

Uganda Railway station, Nairobi, c.1905. According to the Handbook for East Africa 1905, the Railway Goans' sports ground was near the railway station.

Club was often the highlight of their week, the scores enthusiastically reported in the local papers.

Elite Goans referred to themselves as Portuguese, but there were some among them who had spent their formative years in British India, before arriving in East Africa. Crossover identities were experimented with: there was Indo-Portuguese obviously, but briefly there was also the syncretic Anglo-Goan and Anglo-Portuguese. Whatever the transformations they experienced, the twentieth century consolidated their identity in East Africa as uniquely Goan - never Indian - and steadily they began objecting to the term Goanese.

In the founding years of colonial East Africa there was a tenuous Goan-Parsi bond, encouraged by the British for the similarities they perceived between the two ethnicities, and which had its roots in the railway towns of India. At one time, there was a suggestion that Goan and Parsi children should be schooled together. Advertisements appeared requesting either Goan or Parsi clerks. The Oriental Sports Club, inaugurated in 1906 in Mombasa, had as its president, C. M. Dalal and its vice-president, G. Furtado. The intent of this club was to form a bridge between the 'many castes and creeds'. But this kinship dissipated as Goans grew in numbers and prosperity.

Although Lewis Sequeira did not work for the railway and belonged instead to the small contingent of clerks working for the protectorate offices, he played an active role in the Portuguese Cricket Club. His love of cricket would have been a motivating reason to join the club, for he played for them consistently till 1903, and he continued to play cricket, after the Portuguese Cricket Club disbanded, under the new banner of the Goan Cricket Club. Nor was Sequeira shy of assuming the odd role in the dramatic plays the Portuguese Cricket Club put up to entertain the township.

Among the stalwarts of the Portuguese Cricket Club were Leandro de Mello, the assistant clerk at the sub-commissioner's office; A. P. Ferreira, first class 'artizan', a technical post earning a handsome salary of Rs 2,700; D. Franco, first grade accounts clerk; and the musically gifted Zacharias John Fernandes, clerk at the sub-commissioner's office. This pioneering band of men were pillars of early Nairobi: organising church funds, sports tournaments, composing and directing plays and orchestral music. This burst of energy had much to do with being employed by the British civil establishment, in which each man wore many hats and served the community as best they could.

In 1903, at a time when relations between railway and non-railway members of the Portuguese Cricket Club, had become bellicose and the membership had dwindled from forty-two to twenty-five, Harry A. F. Currie took over as railway manager. Currie took a deep interest in the social life of his railway employees. He and his wife entertained extensively; the European Railway Institute experienced a whirlwind of social events under his watch. Little wonder then, that Currie would have been keeping a close eye on the Portuguese Cricket Club. When he was approached about the lack of franchise non-railway members endured, he reasserted the primacy of the railway employees: financial assistance could

Nairobi map, 1920, MPGG1/95, National Archives, Kew. The protectorate subordinate quarters off the Ngara road. By 1911, the Goan Housing Board of Ngara Road quarters had been set up. The Goan sports ground (encircled) is behind the quarters. In 1909, the Railway Goan Institute was formed. In 1911, the Goan Institute acquired a sports ground near Ngara Road, in order to better train for their cricket and football matches. The rivalry between the Railway Goans and the Goan Institute continued to be an impediment towards creating a good cricket team. By 1920, among the Goan teams were the Goan Institute, Railway Goan Institute and the Portuguese Republicans.

only be provided by the railway if management of the club rested with its railway members.

The club floundered all through 1904, bidding the year farewell with a dance at the club's pavilion. Invitations were sent out to all the 'Goan families in Nairobi as well as to the outstations'. Decked with 'flags and bunting', the hall was tastefully decorated by J. C. M. Rebello. The toast for the evening was raised by the 'ever popular Reverend Burke'. A musical quintet directed by Z. J. Fernandes was 'all that could be desired'. It was to be their last hurrah. Six months later, the Goan merchants of Nairobi had declared their intention to form an independent institute.

Julio Marcelo Campos, c.1910-1920. The founding president of the Goan Institute (Nairobi).

'THE BEST EDUCATED AND STRONGEST MEN': THE GOAN INSTITUTE

The Goan Institute of Nairobi epitomised the highpoint of elite culture; that of the erudite, eloquent, multilingual, champagne-drinking and ballroom dancing Goan.

A 1911 anonymous letter appearing in the *Indian Voice* summarised the extent to which Goans were polarised in Nairobi: 'the community is divided into two classes: the educated class and the uneducated or illiterate class. To the former belong such as doctors, clerks, compositors, merchants, mechanics etc. and the illiterate section is principally composed of cooks, tailors, *dhobis*, shoemakers etc. Now these two sections of the community do not intermingle with one and another in social intercourse…In fact, they do not mix'. This severe social segregation based partly on caste but largely on class distinction was woven into the constitution of the Goan institute and would define its internal politics for many decades.

Dr Rosendo Ribeiro was the benevolent benefactor of the Goan Institute, but its founding direction came from Julio Marcelo Campos and Lewis Sequiera. The two would have fraternized as fellow clerks; Campos employed by the Uganda Railway and Sequiera by the protectorate.

It is likely Campos's youthful imagination was coloured by stories of Africa. Two of his brothers, Agapito Campos and J. L Campos, were in South Africa and the latter-mentioned worked for the Central South African Railways. A twenty-two year old Campos had joined the Uganda Railway in February 1898, as a typist in the chief engineer's office earning an annual remuneration of Rs 1500. His family owned a house in Anjuna, Goa, although they drew their *zonn* (dividend revenue from collective ownership of property) from Saligao, which suggests they were *gaunkars* of Saligao. By 1903, Campos was working in the manager's office of the railway. A charming raconteur with a fondness for the ladies and not averse to playing the odd theatrical role on stage, Campos was exceptionally articulate, fond of quoting European writers and thinkers, and innately intelligent. Despite a modest formal education and being almost entirely self-taught, he was soon cast in a leadership role and described by his peers as a 'desirable representative of the Goan community'. He was frequently called upon to address high-ranking British officials and lead delegations. Campos's role has obscured with history but he was in every respect an early civil rights

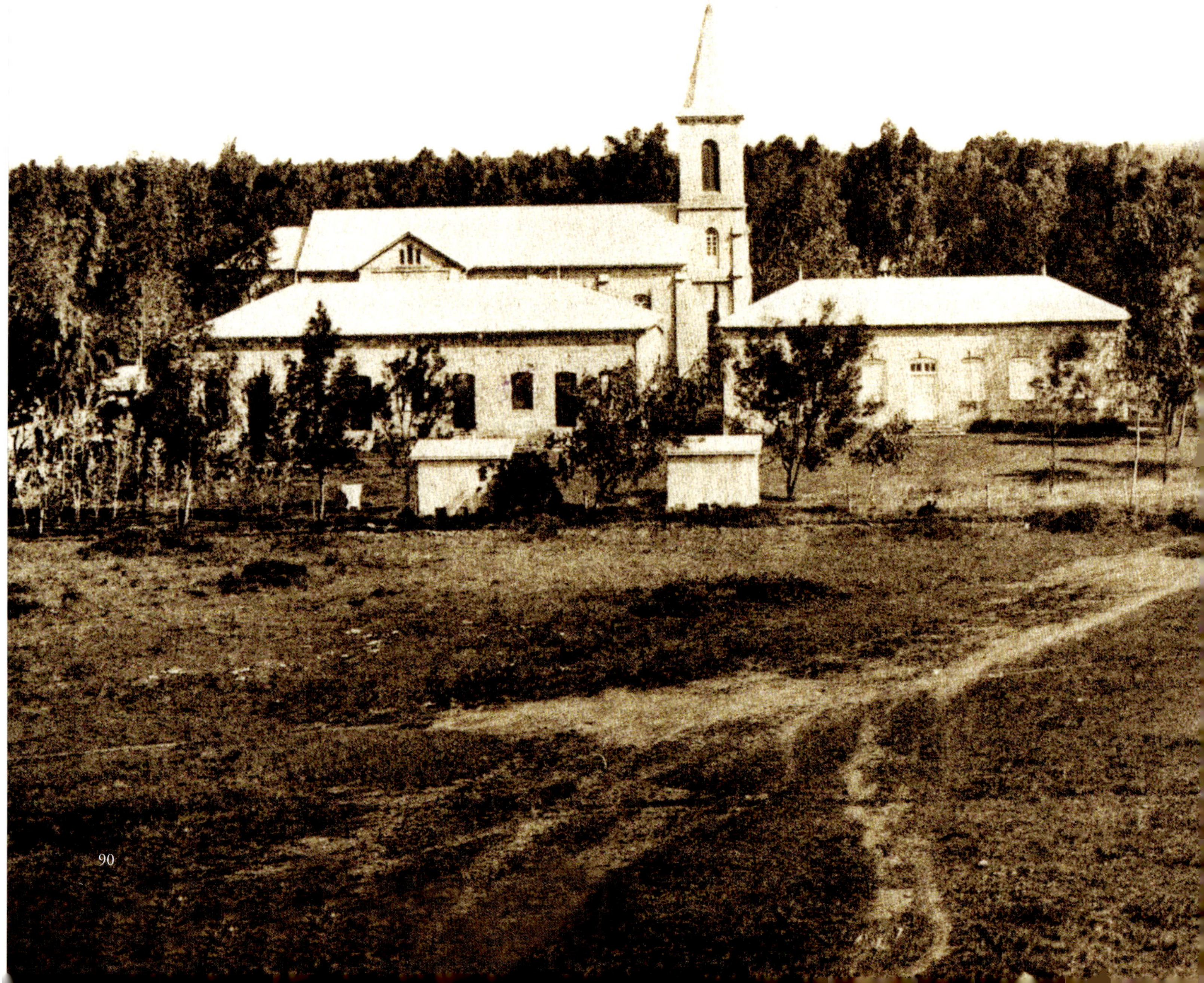

'BEAUTIFUL SANCTUARY LAMP': THE HOLY FAMILY CHURCH

The tireless Bishop Emile Allgeyer had first arrived in Nairobi on the Saturday, 12 August, 1899. Sitting beside him on the train were Brother Blanchard Dillenseger and Father Alain Hémery, both of the Holy Ghost Fathers. They were exhausted, they had been travelling for three days from Voi, but felt strangely invigorated. As the middle-aged Allgeyer hurried from one dirty makeshift tent to the next, trying to convince the young men building the railway of the merits of a Catholic church, it was his Goan congregation of railway employees who rallied around him. After mass held on 20 August, celebrating the feast of St. Joachim, Allgeyer had a meeting with the Goans. In their pious faces he shrewdly caught a glimpse of the future and what would one day become the Holy Family Basilica. They promised to subscribe for the church and petition the chief engineer, George Whitehouse. Allgeyer, a native of Alsace but educated in Ireland, was not a stranger to Goans. On the contrary, he was well acquainted with them. He had officiated at their ceremonies in Zanzibar, presided over their funerals and weddings, and knew them as stout-hearted supporters of the Catholic Church.

Chief Engineer Whitehouse pointed to a stretch of land on his map on which the Catholics could build their church. Plans were drawn up by 1900, but of the Rs 10,000 required amount, an early estimate which was soon revised upwards, only Rs 3,000 was in hand. Meanwhile Goans keen on attending Sunday mass made do with the Traffic office loaned by the railway and converted into a temporary chapel. Father Caysaz had assumed charge of the chapel, holding mass in the morning and benediction service in the evening but had been unable to make much progress in raising funds towards a building. Nonetheless he pursued the project doggedly; a church building fund was created with M. Gallagher appointed as president. Every member of the church was expected to contribute a minimum of Rs 1 per month and subscription lists were sent out.

Two events forced the issue of a building; the railway authorities wanting to reclaim their office space and the despatch of the dynamic Father Thomas Burke in December 1903 to Nairobi. The thirty year old, good-natured Father from Limerick in Ireland, suffering terminally from tuberculosis, immediately

Nairobi Catholic Church, c.1910.

92

Wolfgango D'Cruz, joined the Treasury as junior clerk in 1905. He donated Rs 75 towards the Holy Family Church. In 1906, the year the church was completed, D'Cruz was earning Rs 840 per annum.

endeared himself to his Goan parishioners. Like Allgeyer, he was no stranger to Goans having tended to their pastoral needs in Zanzibar. In Nairobi, he was a familiar figure at Goan celebrations.

Soon after his arrival, Father Burke pointed to the 'bare and ugly walls' of his make-do chapel and urged his parishioners to 'come forward generously with help to build the new church'. He formed the Church Society comprising of Gallagher, R. E. Miller, D. Franco as treasurer and A. P. Ferreria, the last two being Goans, to oversee the plans. By May 1904, a site had been approved by Commissioner Charles Elliot for the church building.

Although white-collar Goans played a crucial role in organising the fund-raising, the choir, the flower arrangements and altar decorations of the Nairobi Catholic church, a no lesser role was assumed by the Goan stewards and tailors towards raising church funds. The tailors maintained they had organised the first high-mass in Nairobi with three priests in attendance and laid claim to forming the first confraternity (an association of lay people promoting Christian charity). St. Francis Xavier, the much loved and venerated saint of Goa, was co-opted by the tailors, and their charities, guilds and clubs were named in his honour. The St. Francis Xavier feast was celebrated right from the inception of the Catholic Church in British East Africa. In 1920, in a rare act of solidarity, the Goan Institute at the request of the Nairobi Goan Tailors' Society, petitioned the Kenya government to declare 3 December, day of St. Xavier's feast, a holiday for Goans. Although unsuccessful in getting the whole day off, they did manage to be excused from work till 10 a.m, allowing them enough time to attend the morning mass.

The building of the church got underway towards late 1904, when Father Kuhn, the architect, arrived along with Brother Simon and four masons. One knowledgeable contemporary letter writer in 1909 estimated the Goans had contributed Rs 13,000 towards the building fund, almost the entire sum required. In August of 1906, the new Holy Family Church was completed standing adjacent to St. Stephen's. The high mass was led by Fathers Kuhn, Burke and Muller. The choir conducted by D'Cruz gave a rousing performance. At the end of the service a record collection of Rs 100 had been taken.

That first Christmas in the new church would have been an exciting time for Nairobi Goans. And they were not disappointed. Bishop Allgeyer arrived at the 'throne' at midnight and the pontifical high mass began at once. The master of ceremonies for the night was S. F. de Souza. The choir was led by D'Cruz and the organ played by Tate. Floral decorations graced the altars and a parishioner had gifted the church a 'beautiful sanctuary lamp'.

It would be the last Christmas the Goans would spend with Father Burke. Less than a year later, in September 1907, Burke died. The town in mourning paid its respects by closing its shops. As his funeral cortege passed through the streets, it was followed by a large crowd of Goans and Europeans.

Wedding day, Nairobi, 1917. Olivet Almeida joined the PWD in 1909. He wed Martha at the Holy Family Church. Martha was Dr Rosendo Ribeiro's niece and known to be a gracious hostess. Olivet was awarded an MBE for his years of dedicated service in the British administration.

SOURCES

Maps (MR), Colonial Office (CO) and Foreign Office (FO) papers, The National Archives, Kew.
Mackinnon (IBEAC) papers, School of Oriental and Africa Studies, University of London, Russel Square, London.
Collected volumes of following handbooks and colonial papers, holdings at British Library, King's Cross.
Handbook for British East Africa, 1905.
Zanzibar Blue Book (1913 – 1917).
Kenya Blue Book (1902 – 1907).
Zanzibar Gazette (1897 – 1919).
East African Standard, Mombasa Times and Uganda Argus (1903 – 1910).
Times of East Africa (1905 – 1907).
Advertiser of East Africa (1907).
The Pioneer (1908).
Indian Voice of British East Africa (1911 – 1912).
East African Chronicle (1920).
Kenya Gazette (1901 – 1910).
Oral Histories of British-Goans project (2001 – 2014), funded by the Heritage Lottery Fund, UK, managed by Selma Carvalho, deposited at the British Library.
Carvalho S, *A Railway Runs Through: Goans of British East Africa*, 1865 – 1980; London, Matador Publications, 2014. Funded by the Heritage Lottery Fund, UK.
Carvalho S, *Into the Diaspora Wilderness: Goa's untold Migration stories from the British Empire*; Goa, Goa 1556, 2010.
Genealogies sourced from the extensive work done by Richard de Souza (unpublished).

IMAGE CREDITS

Image credits
The author gratefully acknowledges the permission granted to reproduce the copyright material in the book. Every effort has been made to trace copyright holders and to obtain permission for the use of copyright material. The author apologises for any errors or omissions in the list below and would be grateful if notified of any corrections that should be incorporated in future reprints or editions of this book. Photographs of individuals featured, have been verified by the family members who have supplied them. While all efforts have been made to ascertain the identities, locations and dates, the author requests to be notified of any inadvertent inaccuracies.
Dhow, A. C. Gomes & Son.
Landing beach, A. R. Pereira de Lord.
Chaiton D'Almedia, ADM188/132/108657, The National Archives, Kew.
View from Zanzibar, de Lord.
Map of Zanzibar, FO 925/7046, survey 1892, printed 1904, The National Archives.
Portuguese Street, p 10, Album 59, Melville J. Herskovits Library of African Studies Winterton Collection, Northwestern University.
John Peter de Souza Bakery, *Zanzibar Gazette*, 1898, The British Library Board.
Roldao Souza and wife, courtesy Marconi de Souza (grandson).
C. R. de Souza store, de Lord.
C. R. de Souza, courtesy Marconi de Souza (great-grandson).
Sultan Military Band, photo 16, box 65, Winterton Collection.
Military medals, courtesy Mina de Souza (great-granddaughter).
Band programme, *Zanzibar Gazette*, 1898, The British Library Board.
View of Zanzibar, J. B. Coutinho.
Dr Luis A. Andrade, p 53, album 3, group 56, Winterton Collection.
Andrew R. Pereira de Lord, courtesy Phyllis Pereira de Lord (daughter) and Joseph Pereira de Lord (nephew).
A. C. Gomes letter, CO323/623/27, National Archives.
De Lord Photo Studios, de Lord.
J. S. Figueira, courtesy Prescilda Preciosa Figueira Border (granddaughter).
J. S. Figueira with staff, Border.
Dr M. F. de Albuquerque, courtesy Ruth Albuquerque (daughter-in-law).
Surgical Hall, de Lord.
Main Road Zanzibar, Ali Pira Harji.
Victoria Gardens, de Lord.
Goan clerk with caravan porters, photo 15, box 65, Winterton Collection.
Nominal Roll, FO2/795, The National Archive.
Mervyn Maciel hunting, both images courtesy Mervyn Maciel.
Gun advertisement, *The Pioneer*, 1908, The British Library Board.
Main Road Mombasa, Coutinho & Sons.
M. R. de Souza advertisement, *The Pioneer*, 1908, The British Library Board.
M. R. de Souza gravestone, Selma Carvalho
Christening, courtesy Benegal Pereira (grandson).
Wedding, courtesy Mervyn Maciel (son).
Ezalda Clara Albuquerque, courtesy Yvonne Dias (granddaughter) & Joe D'Cruz (grandson).
Caetano Jose Dias, courtesy Dias.
Caetano J. Dias with friends, courtesy Dias.
Kibwezi station, Album 6 Nr. 3 (153), Evangelisch-Lutherisches Missionswerk Leipzig e.V.
Augusta Elvira de Souza, p 16, album 1, group 8, Winterton Collection.
Map of Nairobi, MR1/1027/2, 1904, National Archives.
Dr Rosendo Ribeiro on zebra, unknown.
Subordinates quarters Nairobi, p 17, album 2, group 21, Winterton Collection.
Hospital staff Nairobi, p 16, album 2, group 21, Winterton Collection.
Indian Bazaar, D. V. Figueira.
J. A. Nazareth, courtesy Prof. Larry Nazareth (grandson).
Nazareth bros. advertisement, *The Pioneer*, 1908, The British Library Board.
Map of Nairobi, MPGG1/95/3, 1920, National Archives.
Uganda Railway Station Nairobi, D. V. Figueira.
J. M. Campos, courtesy Armand Campos (son).
Map of Nairobi, MPGG1/95/3, 1920, National Archives.
Catholic Church Nairobi, *The Standard*.
Wolfgang D'Cruz, courtesy Betsy Nunes (granddaughter).
Wedding day, courtesy Dr John Almeida (son).
Nairobi society, courtesy Yvonne Dias (granddaughter).

Nairobi society. Standing left C. J. Dias with (unidentified) friends. This picture bears the notation: Nairobi, 2 April, 1926.

95